S0-BMW-630

THE
SEEKER'S
WAY

THE
SEEKER'S
WAY

Cultivating the Longings
of a Spiritual Life

DAVE FLEMING

JOSSEY-BASS
A Wiley Imprint
www.josseybass.com

Copyright © 2005 by John Wiley & Sons, Inc.

Published by Jossey-Bass

A Wiley Imprint

989 Market Street, San Francisco, CA 94103-1741   www.josseybass.com

No part of this publication may be reproduced, stored in a retrieval system, or transmitted in
any form or by any means, electronic, mechanical, photocopying, recording, scanning, or
otherwise, except as permitted under Section 107 or 108 of the 1976 United States Copyright Act,
without either the prior written permission of the Publisher, or authorization through payment
of the appropriate per-copy fee to the Copyright Clearance Center, Inc., 222 Rosewood Drive,
Danvers, MA 01923, 978-750-8600, fax 978-750-4470, or on the web at www.copyright.com.
Requests to the Publisher for permission should be addressed to the Permissions Department,
John Wiley & Sons, Inc., 111 River Street, Hoboken, NJ 07030, 201-748-6011, fax 201-748-6008,
e-mail: permcoordinator@wiley.com.

Jossey-Bass books and products are available through most bookstores. To contact Jossey-Bass
directly call our Customer Care Department within the U.S. at 800-956-7739, outside the U.S. at
317-572-3986, or fax 317-572-4002.

Jossey-Bass also publishes its books in a variety of electronic formats. Some content that appears in
print may not be available in electronic books.

Credits are on page 155.

Library of Congress Cataloging-in-Publication Data

Fleming, Dave

The seeker's way : cultivating the longings of a spiritual life / Dave Fleming.— 1st ed.

  p. cm.

Includes bibliographical references.

ISBN 0-7879-7099-9 (alk. paper)

1. Spiritual life—Christianity. I. Title.

BV4501.3.F578 2005

248.4—dc22   2004019593

Printed in the United States of America

FIRST EDITION

HB Printing   10 9 8 7 6 5 4 3 2 1

Contents

To the Seekers' Group

Kate, Sue, Norma, Mary, Howard, Peg, Sue, Kathy, and Carol

Acknowledgments

The content of this book is close to my soul. For a writer, this is both a good and a dangerous thing. It's always helpful if an author feels fervent about his or her work, yet this proximity and passion can create blind spots in the author and in the book itself. I want to thank my editor, Sheryl Fullerton, for helping me see those blind spots and working with me to overcome them. I know the book is better because of Sheryl.

I also want to thank Mike Mayer, Katie Eggler, Susie McCabe, and Sue Petropulos for reading various sections or drafts of the book. The suggestions you all made were most valuable.

Thanks to my wife, Kelly, for her help in the editing phase. Some people can craft words the way an artist paints a picture, while others can teach the mechanics of grammar that make for good language. My wife can do both. Her help was invaluable. Thank you also Kelly for your constant love and encouragement. I love you. To my sons, Matt and Drew, thanks for your love and the joy you bring to my life. It's amazing to watch as you turn into young men.

Finally, I want to thank a very special group of people who in so many ways embody the spirit of this book. Thanks to the

Seekers' Group, who have been a part of my life for over ten years now. Thank you for sharing your insights and lives with me. The time we've spent reading, thinking, laughing, crying, and growing is a gift I can only savor. I hope somewhere in the book you find something that reveals how you all have shaped me.

THE
SEEKER'S
WAY

CHAPTER I

Introduction

There's a graveyard in my house.

As in other graveyards, headstones mark the resting places of the dead. Some of these deaths go unnoticed; others are more dramatic. Yet the Great Equalizer plays no favorites. The final state is the same for all: dead.

This graveyard is the place where objects that once held a place of honor await the dreaded giveaway bag. The migration of these objects toward the bag begins when they remain on the floor too long. Live objects get picked up, but objects on life support remain on the floor. And if the object is stepped on without regret, you know its time draws nigh.

In light of the fact that dead objects were once honored and full of life, it's always a sad and ironic moment when I step on one of them. I always wonder what its fate will be. Will it find a new home? Should we sell it on eBay? On occasion, one of the dead objects piques my interest again. "Wow, I didn't know I still had this. Maybe I should resuscitate it."

In these moments, I often recall the day we bought a now-dead object. Someone in the family *really* wanted it—no, *needed* it. Often, it was a toy. Seeing the now-dead toy takes me back to a conversation in Aisle 7: "Dad, we really need this . . . oh, please Dad, we won't ask for anything else the rest of the year."

I counter, "What about all the other toys you had to have? You never play with *them* anymore."

Then comes the all-too-familiar reply: "This time will be different."

For a few days, weeks, or maybe even months, the object does hold up its end of the bargain—satisfaction is achieved. Things *are* different. However, in time the migration occurs. The must-have takes its place alongside many other discarded objects of misdirected desire.

As I snap back to the present moment, I shake my head in disappointment that my sons let the must-have object die. But then I notice, right next to the deceased, a dead object of my own. Like father, like son. Like my boys, I'm on the *hunt* for people and things that will satisfy. How about you?

In an attempt to quench desire, we buy what we don't need, schmooze people we don't like, and create personas we hope will make us more powerful, more beautiful, or more . . . whatever. Yet many of these objects of desire end up in the graveyard. Why so many dead objects? What's going on here? What are we looking for?

We are, by nature, seekers.

This drive is at work in all of us. *We seek for what we do not possess.* We cannot deny this drive; nor should we. We all search for people, situations, and circumstances that will yield meaning and hope. We may not always be conscious of this search, but it is always at work within us, like breath. This need to seek motivates our decisions and animates our action. *What* we seek may distinguish us from each other. *That* we seek reveals we are part of the same human family.

Our common need to seek is an intentional part of our design. It is the centerpiece of our existence, placed in us by the Divine Mystery.* It is a beacon, if you will, meant to lead us home—to the ultimate home that is God. The mystery of this home can never be explained, but it can be experienced here and now. Yet because this drive to seek is often skewed by our poor aim, we settle for objects that lose their appeal and die. When our

---

*Divine Mystery is the name I will use often for God. I am in debt to Adrian van Kaam and Susan Muto for the designation.

desire to seek is aimed at the wrong things, it produces stuff for the giveaway bag. All this leads us to ask, "Toward what should we direct our desire to seek?" This is a question for a lifetime and one that animates each day of our existence.

∿ Our Search for Home ∿

The need to seek is connected to a desire to find our home, and our concern in the pages ahead is the continual search for God—in essence, a search for home. We will consider the everyday ways we can seek the Mystery and thereby cultivate a wise and wondrous spirituality. We will not be primarily interested in intellectual beliefs, doctrines, or religious systems.

Even your particular religion is not my concern. Like you, I have intellectual beliefs about the world and life. I have a strong affinity toward certain spiritual ideas and systems. My faith tradition is Christianity. I embrace it as the path home. Yet I have grown uncomfortable with the view that God cannot or will not work in a person's life until that person has embraced my tradition. My aim is not to impose a religion on you but to invite you to a wonder-filled journey toward home.

The journey to God is a continual and paradoxical journey of the spirit. On the one hand, our search leads us home. On the other, the fuel for the search comes from longings that remind us we have not yet arrived. Arrival is not the aim of the spiritual journey. It is the trek that matters most. This paradox exists because our home is not so much a place as it is a path—a *way* more than a *location*. If our home were a fixed location rather than a path, our fundamental drive to search would be negated, and that would violate our design as humans.

As we've seen, we interrupt our search when we pursue lesser things (which end up in the graveyard). But we can also thwart our search when we seek for the sure thing or the sure answer. This kind of preoccupation for surety is a danger for people interested in a spiritual path. We dare not make our faith or our beliefs the final word of the journey, but simply a first step.

∽ In Pursuit of Sure Things ∽

Imagine a math teacher who stands at the front of his class, adjusts his pocket protector, and declares that he is not sure how to do the current lesson, but with the help of the students, answers *might* be discovered.

How confident would you be?

A surgeon, just prior to giving the patient anesthesia, announces, "I'm fuzzy on a few parts of this procedure, but I've seen it done twice."

How secure would you feel?

A pilot, prior to takeoff, alerts the passengers that one of the engines has malfunctioned. "But hey," the pilot continues, "we still have one that works."

What would you do next?

A presidential hopeful proclaims a passion for our country's ambiguity. With nervous hesitation, the candidate squeaks out, "I'm not sure what to do, but over the next four years I'll give it my best shot."

How would you vote?

Much of our world has been built on apparent certainty. We have low tolerance for haziness in our relationships, situations, or circumstances. We want to *know;* we want a sure thing; we feel as though finding a sure thing is a divine right. Now don't get me wrong. The examples I've cited do require a kind of competence and confidence that is appropriate. The real trouble comes when our thirst for certainty permeates every area of life, particularly the spiritual journey home. When we approach the spiritual path with the same solution-driven desire that marks so much of our lives, it inhibits our ability to travel the terrain of the soul.

The irony is that many have turned spirituality into a sure thing, devoid of any questions, doubts, or struggles. Christianity, in many circles, has become like a game show in which all the answers are given before any questions are asked. This does not resonate with the path of Jesus. The narratives about Jesus portray him as one who upset the confident and ignited a childlike wonder in those who could appreciate *not knowing*. The path of Jesus does not lead so much to assurance as to adventure and transformation. This is true of any authentic spiritual journey.

A spiritual life, therefore, is not so much about confidence in concepts that we believe, or even in a place we're headed, but rather about a path we walk and One who is present to the journey. To walk a spiritual path will not lead us to a smug security or a postponement of life until after death. It is a path lined with sacred doubt that pushes us deeper into the present moment. This way invites us to cultivate a seeker's heart that is so often devalued in an answer-driven world. Perhaps this is why we were created to seek. This kind of seeker's heart moves us into the environment of the unknown, where we can embrace the Mystery who does not desire to be explained but longs to be experienced.

∽ The Search and Beliefs ∽

In the pages ahead, I'll talk about the continual search for God and home and about the everyday ways we can seek God. But I am uneasy imposing my tradition on the mass of humanity (as if I could pull that off), so I want to be transparent about my own spiritual life and even wrestle with it in front of you. This desire for transparency flows from an important principle that is essential to an exploration of the seeker's way: *A seeker admits the limits of particular belief systems and acknowledges that God is far bigger than any human being's conceptions.* This principle is essential, because it keeps the seeker humble and pliable along the way. Seekers are not afraid to simultaneously commit to and doubt their beliefs. That makes a seeker's beliefs both firm and supple. It's not that a seeker is without beliefs; rather, intellectual belief is not the center of faith but a necessary and unavoidable part of it. One who can embrace this paradox can walk the way of the seeker.

∿ Longings That Move Us ∿
onto the Seeker's Way

To seek for more than temporary satisfactions or sure answers requires that we understand the role that longings play in our spiritual journey. Longings are unmet desires that move us along, lead us by our heartstrings onto the path home. The longings of the heart initiate and propel us forward; they are the fuel that keeps the search alive in everyday life. In a very deep sense, longings are two-sided. On the one hand, a longing creates a desire to abandon something that no longer animates our life. On the other hand, a longing creates a desire to venture out toward something that will rekindle and reshape life in fresh ways.

A longing places us between the letting go and the reaching out.

It is best to think of longings as movements from something less desirable to something more desirable. The longing to lose weight, for example, often includes a frustration over our current body shape, as well as a hope for one that is leaner and more attractive. Longings are not simply "the hope for something better" but the movement from the lesser to the better. The movement from too much body weight to a leaner body is where we find health. The same is true of the spiritual life. It takes both—the lesser and the better—to create true longing. It is in between what is and what could be that we live a spiritual life.

In this book, we will explore six particular longings that move us along the way of a spiritual life. Each puts us in an in-between place where we yearn to move into a more authentic expression of our lives. The six longings are these:

1. From answers to experience
2. From activity to meaning
3. From control to compost
4. From shadow to substance
5. From performance to expression
6. From segregation to community

Even though the left side of the longing is portrayed as the less desirable part, it doesn't mean that part of the longing is of no use to our search. If for no other reason, the left side of the longing reveals that we want more than that side can give. In that sense we need it. There are moments in life when the left side of the longing is necessary. Answers are at times very important to life. The spiritual path is not primarily nurtured by answers but by experience, not so much by surface activity as by meaning. It is also possible, as we make our way along the path, for the two sides of a longing to merge. In other words, our answers will eventually come out of our experience, and our activity will be infused with meaning. For most of us, the spiritual journey is first a linear movement from one side to the other and then an integration of both. We will keep both ideas in mind as we explore the longings.

∿ Seekers Who Will Make ∿ the Journey with Us

Along the way of our exploration, we will meet *seven seekers* who embody the spirit of the seeker's way. These are people contemporary to the times in which we live. My initial encounters with each of these seven people came through their writings. I was changed by their books, so I invited them to participate in this project. As I wrote the book, I spent time with each of them, listening to their life stories and their ideas about the spiritual journey. You will meet the seekers, one in each of the chapters devoted to exploring the longings.

Here's the order in which you will discover the longings and the seeker or seekers attached to that chapter:

Longing	Seeker
From Answers to Experience	Wayne Teasdale: Catholic monk who works in the field of inter-spirituality
From Activity to Meaning	Alan Jones: Dean of Grace Cathedral in San Francisco
From Control to Compost	Philip Gulley and Jim Mulholland: Quaker pastors
From Shadow to Substance	Lauren Winner: Scholar and author whose writings are reaching a new generation of seekers
From Performance to Expression	Marcus Borg: Jesus scholar and visionary for twenty-first-century Christianity
From Segregation to Community	Joan Chittister: Benedictine nun with a passion for robust spirituality and authentic feminism

The beliefs of these seven seekers differ, as do their ages, gender, and passions. I do not hold them up for their beliefs or philosophies. My effort has been to show how each person you meet embodies the seeker's way in light of one of the six longings. I sought to remain true to the spirit of our interviews, yet the book is more than six interviews. It includes my ideas about the longings of a seeker. I believe the stories of the seven seekers illustrate and round out many of my thoughts, and I add to theirs as well. With this in mind, think of these seekers as contributing a wonderful texture to each chapter and bringing it alive through their insight and example.

A wonderful journey awaits us. The longings we'll explore will help us make this journey toward home with passion and humility. The longings are part of the path that supports you as you walk, so let each longing lead you to a more authentic expression of your spirituality and your life calling.

To the search!

CHAPTER II

From Answers to Experience

Seeker: Wayne Teasdale is a lay monk and mystic.
He wrote *A Monk in the World: Cultivating a
Spiritual Life* and *The Mystic Heart: Discovering a
Universal Spirituality in the World's Religions.* He
teaches religion and spirituality in both academic
and informal settings throughout the world.

My plane was scheduled to leave at 5:50 A.M. I was on my way to Chicago to interview Wayne Teasdale and was looking forward to my time with this unique seeker who has combined the traditions of Christianity and Hinduism. I met the morning with anticipation, knowing that soon Wayne and I would speak about the important movement from fixed answers to emergent experience.

When I mentioned the time of my departure, my wife, who is allergic to early mornings, thought it would be a good idea for me to drive myself and leave the car at the airport. I laughed and agreed. As I packed my things at 4:00 A.M., I drew deeper into the moment and prayed, "Keep me open to the experience of this day."

As I made my way to the airport, the transmission in the car exploded. Well, it didn't actually explode, but it sure felt like it did. In the darkness of the early morning, the car shook with a fierceness that made it difficult to steer. The gears no longer worked, and I made it into a parking lot by driving in neutral. The initial moments of the experience shook me and exposed in me a vulnerability that I'd rather avoid knowing about. Ten minutes later, my morning-resistant wife appeared to take me the rest of the way. As we drove along in the pre-dawn darkness, I remembered my prayer: "Keep me open to the experience of this day." It sounded good at the time, but I wondered what else the prayer might bring.

About seven hours later, I walked into Wayne Teasdale's apartment, which was located in a small lakefront neighborhood in Chicago. As Wayne invited me inside, I was greeted by the sounds, coming from a CD player, of Tibetan bells. Books, articles, and papers lined the walls and occupied the chairs, and all other available surfaces. As a book lover myself, I knew I would like Wayne.

While waiting for him, my eyes landed on a picture of Jesus in the lotus position. This picture confirmed much of what I already knew about Wayne. He is not only a Benedictine but also a *sannyasa*—a monk in the Indian monastic tradition, perhaps the oldest in the world. Its holy men left everything behind to seek the Absolute. Wayne combines this monastic calling with an impressive academic career at universities and seminaries in Chicago, and he serves on the board of the Parliament of the World's Religions. To Wayne, the picture on the wall was more than an image. It was an icon of his calling.

As I talked with this soft-spoken, insightful monk, I could see that he lives out his vocation in the world of people, deadlines, projects, teaching, and suffering. He is indeed *a monk in the world,* living out a deep call he feels to unite the faith traditions of the world into a kind of inter-spirituality. Wayne believes that all traditions share a common ground that can bring them together without denying the real differences found in those traditions. At the heart of this common ground is the mystic or contemplative experience of God. Beyond words, beyond dogma, there is a connection to the Divine that Wayne wants people to know through their experience.

Wayne settled into the chair opposite me. He seemed tired but present. Wayne battled cancer in 2000, and although he has made a remarkable recovery, his heavy schedule before our meeting had taken a toll on him. I was grateful that he was taking time to meet with me, and I determined to be sensitive to his energy level. As it turned out, there was something about Wayne's weariness, my morning car escapade, and this longing that was about to become very important to our time together and my reflections on it.

∿ Moving Beyond Answers ∿

Early in our spiritual journeys, it's fairly common to look for answers. After all, the longing for a spiritual life often starts with questions we've not been able to answer by other means. It's natural then to think the end result of a spiritual life will be answers—answers about God, about the meaning of life, about why we're here. We are prone to search for these answers because they give us something fixed and permanent to hold onto in an uncertain world. Answers settle things and make it possible for us to move forward with confidence, without the need to give those matters much more thought. But spirituality will always take us beyond reason and the answers we thought fixed and permanent to a place of robust and vital experience.

Answers are not altogether bad to pursue, but we have to think of them in an entirely new way: as steps on a ladder that lead us to and through experience. In the last century or so, we have viewed answers as the Holy Grail of science, politics, religion, and business. It wasn't the search for answers but the answers themselves that became central. The search was a necessary evil you had to endure to get to the answers, the way you had to eat your vegetables before the apple pie. Once you had the right answers, you could stop the search.

It is our fascination with fixed and ultimate answers—dogma—that can so easily end the search for Mystery. When answers remove ambiguity and settle all vulnerabilities, those answers become dangerous, and we slip off the path of the seeker. When we use answers to put the Ultimate in a finite box, as if it can be described and contained, stagnation and arrogance result. When we believe we have final answers to all questions, we are no longer open to the experience of life and God. At these times, we are more invested in certainty than in the happenings of the present moment. These two dangers—stagnation and arrogance—will block our vision of God. Our search is hindered or abandoned altogether.

Because of Wayne Teasdale's work in many religious traditions, he understands the snares associated with rigid belief and dogma. As he put it, "It's a much safer world if the world is full of answers, particularly if I believe that my [religious] tradition has all the answers. If that is my view, then there is no reason to talk to anyone else from another tradition or viewpoint."

When I heard Wayne allude to the false security of fixed answers, I knew he was right. How easy it is to create a world that shields me from the reality of my condition. In the end, however, there's no denying that condition.

∿ Denying Our Vulnerability ∿

We are, by nature, vulnerable.

And it doesn't take much to reveal our vulnerability. A broken-down car at 4:15 A.M. did the trick for me. An unwanted phone call from a doctor reveals our frailty. The painful words of a spouse's wayward intention will uncover it. There is no end to the ways in which we are vulnerable. A single moment can move our lives from confidence and competence to desperation and uneasiness, from calmness and certitude to pounding heart, shaking hands, and a soul crying out in pain. These unwanted circumstances of life, which we could all reveal like scars from childhood, are not what make us vulnerable. Rather, they simply reveal that we *are* vulnerable. The troubles that assail us pull back the covers on our illusions of safety and sufficiency.

Of course, as humans we are good at pulling those covers right back up to our chins and continuing to deny realities that make us afraid or uncomfortable. Like the quintessential four-year-old who shields her eyes or ears to deny trouble, we convince ourselves that if we don't admit our vulnerability, we aren't really susceptible to it. We construct our daily lives to insulate ourselves from our weaknesses, and we are often shocked when those frailties poke through our walls of resistance. Spirituality that promises fixed and final answers to the profound questions of human life is too often another attempt to hide from these inner and outer frailties.

∿ Accepting Vulnerability ∿

Acceptance and recognition of vulnerability are essential to authentic spirituality. Genuine spirituality will always move us deeper into our original nature, which is an odd mix of glory and frailty. It's easy to live on the glory side. We want to appear confident, in control, and worthy of adulation. It's quite another thing to embrace the frail and weak side of our nature. This is exactly what vital spirituality requires.

Recognizing the frailty of our humanity is part of finding the pathway to a richer life. Wayne put it this way: "The movement from answers to experience is also the movement from security to vulnerability. If we honor our vulnerabilities, those weak places can ground us in virtues like compassion, peace, and gentleness."

Many people say the quality of their spiritual life is enriched during times of pain and sorrow. As we look back on these moments of great vulnerability, we see the shape of our lives transformed.

The experience of vulnerability deepens as we move closer to the original sense of the word. The Latin root for vulnerability, *vulnero,* means "to wound." A deep spirituality is therefore open to the wounds that, in fact, mature and refine. These wounds are not meant to imply a kind of masochistic approach to spirituality. Rather, to allow for vulnerability—for wounds—is to allow my nature to express itself for what it is. I do not know everything. I am not in control. My answers will only take me so far.

Frailty without rigid answers makes us more receptive to the search for a life filled with wonder and compassion. Paradoxically, even though we may hope for a spiritual life that will release us from vulnerability, it will not. In fact, it will lead us deeper into it, because there we see our need for change and the grace to live a radically free yet responsible life.

Someone who is open to the spiritual path is often open because he or she has exhausted the pursuit of stability and certainty through material, social, familial, or political paths. These paths are important, and they have their own reward, but they never seem quite enough. Alone, these paths may only reveal our transcendent ache. Many spiritual seekers turn to God in hopes that God will become the ultimate fix, or answer, like the TV character of my youth, Mr. Wizard. He could remove anxiety and color life the shade of a rose. "If anything should take away weakness, it should be God," goes the thinking. How easy it is to believe God is little more than an answer dispenser who proves me right and keeps me safe from the harsher realities of life.

All of this can lead us to believe religious answers will make the difference where lesser answers have failed, but the fact is, they won't. I recently spoke with a woman who viewed the Bible as the ultimate answer to every question. Yet something about her view didn't ring true to her. She was seeking for a way to honor her sacred text but allow the world to be bigger than that text. As we talked, I noticed her vulnerability increase. For a moment, I thought she was going to engage me in the conversation, but then she got too close to the need for certainty and declared, "Look, I just need you to reassure me that the Bible is God's truth . . . because I need *something* to be sure about." She was not comfortable with the idea that the Bible might not be what she wanted it to be, at least in part, because her view of the Bible was her shield against the vulnerability of unanswered questions. I know how this woman feels.

I'm just as guilty of memorializing my own answers because, well, they're *my* answers. Better yet (I may think), they're God's answers. Having God on my side creates a feeling of security, and security is an end state where I feel no vulnerability. Once-and-for-all answers can actually move us in the opposite direction of the seeker's path. They can lead to a smug satisfaction and, at worst, outright pride and prejudice. For those on the seeker's way, vulnerability can be a healthy state that moves us deeper into the experience of the present moment. I found that out as my interview with Wayne Teasdale unfolded.

∿ Entering into the Experience ∿

My interview with Wayne didn't begin the way I had thought it would. It was scheduled for 3:00 P.M., but it was 3:30 or later before we found each other. Also, because Wayne must follow a strict diet, it was important that he prepare and eat some food before we got too far into the interview. So after our initial greeting, Wayne prepared his meal and I waited, eyeing the picture of Jesus in lotus position in the corner. Once the interview began, he had some important calls to take, so again I waited while he spoke on the phone. Then after we had spent about forty-five minutes on the topic, I could tell Wayne was tired. I suggested a break. I don't know whether I suggested this out of compassion for Wayne's situation or guilt that I had added one more thing to his schedule. But he was appreciative, and I left to sit in my car while he took a thirty-minute nap.

As I sat in my car, I felt disappointed. I wasn't sure the interview was accomplishing what it should. Would I have the material I needed for the chapter? Was this a bad idea? My mind flitted from one negative thought to another until it was finally time to talk to Wayne again. As I sat there, I decided I should try something different with the second part of our interview—a new approach that would help me worry less about results and just be present to our time together.

After Wayne's nap, I left my tape recorder and notes in the car, and the two of us walked along the lakefront outside Chicago. We talked about Jesus, religion, inter-spirituality, and life. We walked in silence. We stopped on occasion to talk to one of Wayne's former students or to listen to the birds that occupied the trees around the shore. In short, we entered the experience of being together in those moments. As Wayne and I walked, I realized I didn't need answers from him; I just needed to be *with* him. Ironically, it was from this more relaxed place of experience that many important insights emerged in our conversation. And those insights led us deeper into the experience of the moment.

This led me later to an important question: *Is it possible that when answers come out of our experience with God, they become insights for the journey?* And is it also possible that those insights (enlightened answers) cause us to desire more of the very experience that produced them? Rather than obsess on the already discovered answer, we hunger for the experience that led to the answer. For life is not in the answer but in the experience.

Three or four weeks after my time with Wayne, I realized that what I needed most from Wayne was *not* the answers to my questions but his vulnerable presence that marked the experience. I realized that Wayne himself was what I needed, because through Wayne's presence I recognized my own vulnerability about the interview and my ability to see this project through to the end. My vulnerability drew me deeper into the experience and led me to new insights, new answers, and new questions. For this is vulnerability's gift: it invites us deeper into the present moment where life awaits us.

Early in my time with Wayne, I was fidgety because my eyes were on the answers Wayne could give me rather than the experience we could share. I was pulled away from the very moment I longed to experience. What a picture of my life.

The interview with Wayne revealed my need to make my own move from answers to experience. I was most concerned that Wayne provide me with great thoughts and quotes (which, by the way, he did). But it was harder for me to enter the experience. As the interview lurched along through Wayne's lunch, his meditation, his nap, my sojourn in the car, and our walk along the lake, I felt varying degrees of vulnerability. I wanted and needed answers. I had a book to write. Yet at an intuitive level, I knew this attitude would only hinder the rest of my time with Wayne.

∿ Stepping Away from Answers ∿

Perhaps the first step away from an answer-driven spiritual life is to view answers in a new way. What if answers became more like doorways into another space where the search can continue? Instead of ending the search with finite and rigid answers, these new insights can move us deeper into life's realities. For example, I believe that God exists. It is an answer I believe I've discovered through seeking. However, a belief in God was never meant to create a smug sufficiency but rather to deepen my pursuit of the Divine. A belief in God is not an answer that ends the search but one that makes it possible to broaden and deepen the search. Let me illustrate.

Find a surface near you. It could be a table or a section of the floor beneath you or even the page you now have before you. Imagine that on the surface you could hold all the mysteries and knowledge of God. All of it! It could all be contained on that surface. Now let me tell you something about me. I'm a fairly intelligent person. I have a doctorate (a real one, not the mail-order kind). I've read broadly and deeply and have studied for many years. I'm also open to the experience of things beyond my knowledge, which has increased my insight over the years. Now that you know this about me (and, believe me, I could tell you more), how big a circle would you draw to represent my knowledge, wisdom, and understanding on the entire surface you've chosen (which again represents all knowledge and mystery)? Are you laughing yet? Would you even make a mark on the page? Trust me, you wouldn't.

Now include yourself in the next circle. If you and I combined our knowledge and understanding, how big would you now make the circle? Are we both laughing? How about if we include all the people both of us know? How big would the circle be? Oh, just throw all of humanity in there. Now how big is that circle?

No matter how much we know, it is still minuscule in light of all the wonders, mysteries, and knowledge of the Divine. Answers alone are not the point. But insights—or what I call enlightened answers—are portals to a deeper experience of God rather than the final word on the One who can never be explained. With each round of insight, we are invited to go deeper into the Mystery where our old insights can be reformed and renewed. More important, we are invited to simply be with God in a relationship that isn't based on what we can figure out but what we can share.

∽ Describing Experience ∽

The experience of life and God that we are exploring in this chapter is often beyond words, but it is still important to try to describe it. Language has its limitations, yet it is a primary vehicle by which we can express matters of the heart. We've all had the experience of reading something that put our feelings into just the right words. Language that resonates allows us to enter and cultivate our spirituality in deep and meaningful ways. Of course, we must not allow our language to become rigid answers that end the search. With that in mind, let's look at two words that will help to describe experience that leads to the Mystery: *dimensional* and *transformational.*

Experience Is Dimensional

I use the word *dimensional* to describe the longing for experience because it suggests that experience is an actual layer—a dimension—of life we can either enter or completely miss. A helpful illustration of "experience as dimension" is 3-D photography. You come upon a picture that looks like nothing more than a series of random dots, like splattered paint on a canvas. But as you stare at the dots, your eyes move in and out of focus until a 3-D image pops out at you. Amazing! The experience of the picture is dimensional *if you know how to look at it.*

In any given moment of life, the dots of the experience may seem random, disconnected, and unimportant. But if we know how to enter the moment with the right eyes, a deeper and richer experience emerges. We see the same dots as always, but something deeper reveals itself because of a more relaxed and less rigid entrance into that moment. Rigid answers will often keep us from this deeper dimension because our answers narrow our vision. Widening and deepening our view depends on the posture of our hearts and the sensitivity of our intuition and imagination.

In Wayne's book *A Monk in the World,* he writes about an experience he had with a rose:

> It all came together for me while I was contemplating a rose bush in my front yard in West Hartford, Connecticut. In watching the bush over time, I realized that reality, like the

rose, is a process of growth, or unfolding. Just as the rose is more than any one stage of its development—bud, stem, or bloom—so life and reality are more than any one moment of time or experience. What is real is not just its moments of duration but also the totality of the process of manifestation in time.[1]

Wayne saw the physical rose, but then that physical rose drew him to a metaphorical place of meaning: the picture popped out of the dots. This other dimension of experience is how we encounter and engage the Beyond. Behind the obvious, below the surface lurks greater significance. We've all experienced a moment when something as ordinary as a rose becomes a portal to greater meaning. The physical reality takes us to a spiritual reality where our hearts connect to the Mystery.

The poet William Blake conveyed the same idea in the first four lines of "Auguries of Innocence":

To see a world in a grain of sand,
And a heaven in a wild flower,
Hold infinity in the palm of your hand,
And eternity in an hour.[2]

This vision combines what is temporal and what is eternal. When Jesus spoke of eternal life, he was referring less to a life that would go on indefinitely and more to a life lived from the dimension of eternity. We might say that eternity is God's dimension. This dimension was never meant to be thought of as separate from the dimension of the tangible and concrete. Eternity can be seen in a grain of sand or in any hour of the day. Eternity can be seen in the glance of a friend or the suffering of a loved one.

Jesus often spoke of this dimension as the kingdom of heaven—the place we touch the Mystery's life and that which is timeless. This is heaven on earth, and it's available to anyone, but it does require us to cultivate the right eyes if we are to see. Because many in Jesus' day could not see this dimension, he told stories to illustrate what a person influenced by this dimension looked like. Here's an example:

> There was once a man traveling from Jerusalem to Jericho. On the way he was attacked by robbers. They took his clothes, beat him up, and went off leaving him half-dead. Luckily, a priest was on his way down the same road, but when he saw him he angled across to the other side. Then a Levite religious man showed up; he also avoided the injured man. A Samaritan traveling the road came on him. When he saw the man's condition, his heart went out to him. He gave him first aid, disinfecting and bandaging his wounds. Then he lifted him onto his donkey, led him to an inn, and made him comfortable. In the morning he took out two silver coins and gave them to the innkeeper, saying, "Take good care of him. If it costs any more, put it on my bill— I'll pay you on my way back."[3]

The Samaritan had eyes to see beyond the surface. The religious and important people who passed by saw what they wanted to see; none saw the God-dimension of eternity. Only the Samaritan saw that, and it altered not only his vision but his action.

It is not always easy to see beyond the obvious. Many aspects of modern life seem to prevent it. In *A Monk in the World,* Wayne writes, "This capacity has been obscured in the last century by our Western preoccupation with frenetic work, scientific analysis, rational discourse, and technology."[4]

We have been stripped of the ability to enter into the experience of the moment and simply be in it. We seem to think that an experience is only valid if it leads to answers, proofs, results, and quantifiable knowledge. Yet so much more awaits us when we loosen our grip and open our eyes.

Experience Is Transformational

The other quality of experience that is important to our exploration is transformation. True experience always changes me. As I journey into the dimensions of reality and Spirit, I will be made new in some manner. The spiritual path challenges me to grow, face illusions and vulnerabilities, and join God in a process of reforming those frailties. Wayne put it nicely when he told me, "A seeker is one who has made a commitment to her own transformation."

This is perhaps one reason we may not always see this dimension of experience. Transformation can be hard. It is certainly not the easy road in most cases. To face our own egos and move to a more authentic self can be arduous. Give us answers instead; that's the easy way.

Experience of the eternal is not like the Disneyland ride, "It's a Small World After All." The experience of the seeker is not some jolly journey that demands nothing while it delivers painless change and temporary delight. The experience invites us to see into ourselves—our insecurities, dysfunctions, prejudices, and blind spots—and commit to an ongoing process of change. The process turns dysfunctions into virtues like peace, awareness, compassion, and joy. These desirable qualities turn us outward until our personal experience becomes the basis for compassionate action.

∾ Cultivating Experience ∾

As with all of the longings we will examine in this book, the movement from answers to experience requires intentional cultivation. To be open to the epiphanies of the Mystery in our experience of life means we are living our lives in a receptive manner. We cannot force this dimension, but we can prepare to see and touch it through purposeful practice. In each chapter, we will explore meaningful practices that open us to each longing. Some of these practices require us to set aside time and resources, while others are easily integrated into our everyday lives.

When we think about a practice that would help us cultivate the dimension of experience and move us away from rigid answers, we need to look no further than pilgrimage. For many in our society, the word *pilgrimage* has lost its meaning. Understanding a pilgrimage and participating in one opens me to both the dimensional and transformational aspects of experience.

∿ Deepening the Longing ∿

Going on a pilgrimage is a spiritual practice that can assist us in the movement from answers to experience. When we hear the word *pilgrimage,* it may evoke highly religious visions of a person making a trek to, say, Mecca. Though this is one type of pilgrimage, a broader view will help us embrace the practice in real life.

A pilgrimage is a microcosm of a spiritual life because, during the physical journey, the aim is to deepen the experience of the Mystery as one travels. It is a journey in which the traveler is open to the dimension of the eternal and the transformation that results. All stripes of religious traditions value and encourage pilgrimage. This common desire for a sacred journey is, in part, due to the way it connects the traveler to the experience of life.

A pilgrimage is a good pathway into experience as I've described it, because we tend to have different eyes and heightened anticipation when we set off on a sacred adventure. Not to mention the fact that a pilgrimage can often increase our vulnerability because we are in unknown environments where normal answers don't suffice. All this heightens our connection to and desire for the Mystery as we travel.

In *A Monk in the World,* Wayne relates a story of an overnight pilgrimage to the top of Sri Pada, or Adam's Peak in Sri Lanka, where he climbed through the night and watched the sun rise as he reached the top. I won't recount the entire story, which you can read in his book, but suffice it to say that this overnight pilgrimage had all the elements of the experience the seeker longs to enter. It was more than a journey to the top of a mountain. The journey itself deepened Wayne's experience of himself, God, and nature. It brought Wayne close to his own ego and his need to change. It was dimensional in that the eternal was tangible as Wayne climbed, not so much in dramatic ways but in subtle-but-powerful messages. Wayne was transformed by the experience. He came off the mountain different and more compassionate. This is pilgrimage at its best.

Of course, this experience can help us beyond the moments of the pilgrimage. It can become a new way of viewing everyday life. Each day becomes an opportunity to know God, an opportunity to seek God as we make the trek. Each day we can touch the eternal and be transformed by it. As we make a literal journey, we take the spirit of the pilgrimage back into the routines of the everyday. Soon every day can be marked by the seeker's way.

If you've never taken a pilgrimage, a few ideas may help to maximize the journey. First, it's important that first attempts be short. To embark on a forty-day fast in the deserts of Egypt may turn your first adventure into a nightmare. Start small and work your way to more significant time periods. The aim is not the length but the potency of the journey.

When I lived in Maryland, I worked at a counseling center in Northern Virginia. Some days I had long periods of time in between clients, so I would drive, or sometimes walk, to the nearest park or Catholic church (Catholic churches are a great place to meditate). These times became mini-pilgrimages, more because of the posture of my heart than the dramatic nature of the location.

Your first few pilgrimages can be just as short and can even be tied to your routine.

At some point, you may want to take a more significant pilgrimage to a particular site in the world. One day I hope to visit Ireland. I love Celtic spirituality and want to experience it firsthand. This will take some significant planning, so in the meantime I make smaller moments that open me to the experience of the Mystery in powerful ways.

As I made my way around the country to meet with the seekers in this book, that trip became a pilgrimage of sorts. In fact, I decided to create this sense each time I made a trip to meet with one of them. The result was that my heart was far more open to the moments I enjoyed with each person. The experience was enriched by my view of the journey. This is the mind-set we need. Imagine what could happen if it became the mind-set of everyday life.

When you take a pilgrimage, don't fill it with too much activity. The aim is to create space for the experience of the eternal; making such a space keeps surface activity to a minimum. Take a journal and perhaps a sacred text that speaks to your heart, and then simply be and listen as the journey unfolds. You will likely encounter your vulnerability along the way. This is part of the adventure you need not avoid. Learn to listen to the messages about your ego, your identity, your relationships, and your vulnerabilities. Those messages will ripple for days, weeks, and months after the pilgrimage.

Notes

1. Teasdale, W. *A Monk in the World*. Novato, Calif.: New World Library, 2002, pp. 7–8.

2. The poem was first published by Dante Gabriel Rossetti in his edition of Gilchrist's *Life of William Blake*, 1863. It was edited from a manuscript in fair draft written by Blake, probably during his stay at Felpham (1800–1803), and later known as the Pickering manu-

script, from a Mr. B. J. Pickering who bought it and published an edition of it, more accurate than Rossetti's, in 1866.

3. Peterson, E. *The Message*. Colorado Springs, Colo.: Navpress Publishing Group, 2002 (Luke 10:30–36).

4. Peterson, 2002, p. 6.

CHAPTER III

From Activity to Meaning

Seeker: Alan Jones is dean of Grace Cathedral in San Francisco. He is responsible for the oversight of the church's many ministries and represents the church to the world at large. He is also the primary teacher at the cathedral's many weekend services. Jones is author of numerous books, including *Soul Making: The Desert Way of Spirituality* and *Living the Truth.*

In the old movie *Modern Times*, Charlie Chaplin plays an assembly-line worker who tightens screws onto machine parts as they move past him on a conveyer belt. As time passes, Chaplin performs the same motion with a number of comical twists. At certain points, he continues the motion, even though he's no longer near the assembly line at all. The motions continue, even while Chaplin's on break. He's hypnotized by the activity. You can sense the dread of the repetition that drives Chaplin to distraction and frustration.

The first time I saw this movie, it struck me that Chaplin's assembly line could be a metaphor for a dread that can overtake us—a kind of meaninglessness in the motion. What Chaplin meant as silent satire is too often how we move through the course of a day. When this kind of empty routine defines us, we grow hollow on the inside and stale on the outside.

Thomas Kelly, a twentieth-century Quaker, wrote about this tension:

> We're weary and breathless. And we know and regret that our life is slipping away, with our having tasted so little of the peace and joy and serenity we are persuaded it should yield to a soul of wider caliber. . . . Strained by the very mad pace of our daily outer burdens, we are further strained by an inward uneasiness, because we have hints that there is a way of life vastly richer and deeper than all this hurried existence, a life of unhurried serenity and peace and power. If we could only slip over into that Center![1]

Kelly's penetrating comments reveal both the frustration of meaningless motion and the desire of many seekers: to infuse activity with meaning that comes from the center. We long for the grace that enables us to slip into the place of peace and focused energy in the midst of daily activities—the place where divisions between things sacred and things tangible vanish. This is where true potency lives, where we are enlivened from the center to the edges of our existence.

For too long, many of us have lived with a division that makes our daily activity less than the miracle it truly is. This separation causes us to miss the holy in the utterly ordinary. It also creates a need for one turbo-charged experience after another in order to keep life interesting and worthwhile. All the while, the miraculous remains hidden in the mundane.

The movement from activity to meaning is not a negation of motion but a shift in the quality of that motion. As we learn to find meaning in the moment, vacant habits are once again infused with passion and wonder. The simplest of moments, from the glance of a friend to laughter shared over a meal, becomes a portal through which we touch the Mystery and find appreciation for the present moment. We are blessed to simply be in the activity without the need for enhancements. The sacred in the ordinary is enough.

This longing toward meaning in the moment is similar to the zoom lens on a camera. Every day, we have the opportunity to zoom in on events and situations and live out experience in the way we explored in the last chapter. When we are awake to the "sacred infused in the daily," we find meaning in even the simplest experience.

In this longing for meaning, we want to experience the fullness of life in each and every moment. We long to mine life's fullness as it occurs. All things we do matter and are expressions of divine goodness and beauty. Without this view of activity, daily life looks too much like Chaplin's motion—a place we long to avoid.

I rose early and made my way into the city of San Francisco, where I was to meet Alan Jones. Beyond his many responsibilities at Grace Cathedral, Alan has another gift that I discovered many years ago. His ability to communicate his heart and mind through the written word has captivated me for years. In the hotel the night before our meeting, I pulled out several of Alan's books that I had brought along for the interview. These books had become my friends. Over the years, I've been impressed with Alan's rare blend of candor, courage, and true conviction. His is not the sappy religious kind of conviction that leaves one reeling but a type that shuns easy answers and insists on a vibrant and genuine faith.

After I leafed through many of my favorite passages, I came upon an example of this candid conviction:

> I want a kind of Christianity that can be embraced with both passion and intelligence. And in case the reader assumes that I am advocating some watered-down stuff, let it be known that I want nothing of "morality tinged with emotion." I want a gutsy, old-fashioned, demanding, religion with no compromise and no nonsense. I want a great deal.
>
> Often, I feel as yet, I have nowhere to lay my head. The heartiness of fundamentalist, charismatic, or evangelical brands of Christianity are [sic] unattractive to me, as is the legalism of certain brands of Catholicism and Protestantism. I have no wish to be judgmental. All I want to do is make clear some of the things I cannot live with.[2]

After rereading those words, I wondered what my time with Alan would yield. Alan had, through his writings, increased my own courage to seek and my own resolve for a robust faith. Soon I would sit across from a man who had become an icon in the search for the Mystery. I closed the book, and my expectations for the coming interview increased. As I sat in the hotel room swirling the ice in my cup, I had no idea that my time with Alan was not the only place where meaning awaited me. The day to come had more in store.

I put my glass down and checked MapQuest for the Starbucks nearest to Grace Cathedral. It was only five blocks away. Perfect. I had it all planned: I'd park the car near the cathedral and make my way on foot to the other cathedral (Starbucks). Of course, not being from San Francisco, it didn't enter my mind to consider whether those five blocks would be downhill or uphill. They ended up being both.

The walk in the city was good because it put me in touch with the life that awakens there every day. As I passed people on the street, I was reminded that deep within us all there is a desire that our days be meaningful, that our activity matters in and beyond the moment in which it occurs. I was also aware that the desire for meaning could easily be lost in the rush of this new day. I wondered if the people around me would be able to find the meaning hidden in the circumstances that were about to unfold. I wondered the same for myself.

Inside Starbucks, my people-watching continued. I noticed high-powered executive types revving up for the day. Others near me seemed weary, anxious, or excited. Some people made plans; some people changed plans; some talked of the dread of their jobs. Still others scanned the newspaper, perhaps looking for new jobs. A few people found humor in a newspaper article or a passerby. And then there was the couple just to my left whose mutual infatuation stretched each moment into a lifetime of bliss. Like a steady heartbeat, the invitation to meaning pulsed through the moment and the people present to it. I longed for eyes to see the wonder at work in this simple frame.

The size and beauty of Grace Cathedral overwhelmed me. I've been around large churches my entire life, but the cathedral is unique for more than its size. Built in the architectural style of a medieval cathedral, the ceilings are high and the expansive spaces make one feel appropriately small. As I entered, the building took my breath away. This is part of the motive behind the design. The cathedral is meant to give those who enter a sense of the vastness and limitlessness of God.

At the back of the cathedral was a rather large labyrinth (a labyrinth is an ancient tool used to support and nurture prayer) that consists of large circular patterns placed on the floor; participants can walk on it and experience it as a metaphor for the journey of life. As one follows the twists and turns of the spherical design, it creates a sense of movement toward and away from the center and of the surprises that come as the journey unfolds. It is a sacred and yet ordinary trek. One need only enter the process with openness and receptivity to experience its powerful lessons. Meaning emerges in the surrender to the walk itself.

Perfect, I thought. I have enough time before my interview with Alan to walk the labyrinth. This walk, though different from my earlier walk in the city, yielded insights that would shape my interview with Alan and speak to me about my own desire for meaning. (As it turned out, the insights were not at all what I'd anticipated, but more on that later.) After I had walked the labyrinth, I made my way across a common area and found the cathedral offices. I was ushered into a sunny, book-filled sitting room just off Alan's main office. The space was kept meticulously, and I had the sensation that far more important people than I had occupied the seat on which I now sat.

Alan appeared on time, greeting me with his inimitable British accent. I was impressed and a bit taken. British accents are a weakness of mine. I tend to confer brilliance on anyone with an English tone. Alan could have read me the newspaper, and I would have deemed it an inspiring moment. However, my awareness of Alan's accent would soon fade as I came in contact with something much more important: his life. From the moment he walked in the door, I sensed a depth in him that I wanted to know more about. As Alan sat down, there was a deep sense of appreciation and gratitude emanating from his soul. His gaze was full of compassion, and he seemed intent on being very present to our time. Alan conveyed to me through his posture, words, and actions that this interview was important for him. He not only wanted to share his heart but he wanted to learn and seek with me as well. There wasn't a shred of pretense—just openness to the Mystery, the moment, and what we could discover together.

After Alan and I got to know each other and spoke of our mutual desire to be seekers of the Mystery, we moved into our dialogue about meaning-filled activity. Early in this conversation, Alan said, "Finding the meaning means that we actually show up at our own life. So much of the time we're not present to our own lives."

Yes, I thought. This is what I had hoped for earlier as I walked the city and the labyrinth. This is what I had wondered for myself and for those around me. Were we present to the life coursing through the early-morning rush? Had we shown up?

To show up at one's life seems an odd way to describe the pursuit and discovery of meaning, yet that is exactly what is required and often what is missing. Perhaps the motion in the Chaplin movie could best be described as life*less*. This is what Alan had revealed in his comment. We are too often not alive in the midst of our doing. Too much activity is done without heart or passion. Though it pains us to think we might live in this manner, an honest evaluation of our lives would reveal that our activity is often devoid of passion and meaning. When our essence does not infuse our activity, we lose touch with the present moment, and a hole in the soul begins to form. We can deny this hole through busyness or sophisticated distractions, but in the end the hole reminds us of something we've lost and something we ache to rediscover.

Why is it easy to lose touch with ourselves during the day? The question haunted me as I sat across from Alan. Then I realized that the question often haunts me in the corners of my life. It sneaks up on me when I least expect it and invites me to face my own numbness toward life. Something is missing. Could that something be me?

∿ Missing in Action ∿

We lose meaning in life when we divide our actions into the mundane and the significant, convincing ourselves that we only need to show up for the significant moments. The mundane rest of our lives does not, we think, require us to be truly present, so we simply survive it, doing all those insignificant things we must do that yield little true meaning. We eat, sleep, drive to work, and pay bills, and then do it all again the next day. Imagine all these deeds, and many others, passing by you on the conveyer belt of action. You and I, as dutiful employees of life, put A into B, A into B, A into B—again and again. As we do these deeds day after day, we are prone to lose touch with ourselves in the doing. Words like *mindless* and *heartless* could describe most of our waking hours.

Can you remember when your job enlivened you? Can you remember when you could only dream of the job you now take for granted? Maybe early in your career, you saw your job as a way to fulfill a call or further a cause close to your heart. Remember when your job challenged you to grow and stretch toward new personal horizons? There was anticipation and possible development around every corner, but maybe now your vocation is more a way to get a paycheck than fulfill a passion. Perhaps the fire is gone; the desire to grow has waned. Now you thank God when it's Friday. What happened? What did you lose?

How about something as simple as driving a car? Remember the first day you drove a car? Remember how you thought you'd never be old enough to sit behind the wheel? The day would simply never arrive. Can you recall how your heart pounded when you first felt the power and mobility a car provided? You were free to go places and do things once completely beyond your grasp. You memorized the laws of your state and developed a feel for the road. You begged shamelessly to use your parents' car while they held their breath and prayed. That was no insignificant moment. It represented a new kind of liberty and responsibility. Do you still feel that joy? Or is driving simply a necessary evil to get you to the job you no longer enjoy? What happened? How do we lose the significance of these simple situations, relationships, and events that once brought great joy?

Maybe it's not your job or the simple actions like driving but your passion for learning that has dwindled. Or your commitment to a deep and central relationship has grown stale through a lack of heart-filled attention. The sad reality is that familiarity can indeed breed discontent. The sacred meaning once accessible in these moments and relationships becomes hard to recover. Soon it can be hard to believe anything sacred exists. The joy found in the simplest of deeds can be paved over with drudgery and empty routine.

The more our daily actions become mundane and therefore unimportant, the more difficult it is to find meaning in the present moment. Perhaps this is why we run after graveyard trinkets. These shiny lures seem to provide a temporary worth we no longer find in our everyday deeds. Of course, the disappointment when a trinket fails to live up to our expectations can be enormous. Not only do we finally discover the hollowness of the trinket but we have the nagging fear that nothing will ever bring meaning. This can be a very dark place.

Seekers long to recapture the meaning in the mundane because they sense that significance emerges from the ordinary rather than from outside it. The "ordinaries" of life are not to be avoided or hurried through in order to get to the good stuff. They are where the good stuff abides. The simplest of actions brings the possibility of meaning, if we know how to look for it. The ability to look for meaning in the mundane requires us to understand an overlooked quality of the mundane.

When you read the stories in the New Testament about Jesus, you find this sacred-in-the-ordinary practice at work in his life and relationships. Jesus found significance and sacredness in the voices of small children and in the weariness of people beaten down by cultural dysfunction. He drew significance out at parties, funerals, religious celebrations, and time spent searching for the best place to fish. Most re-enactments of Jesus' life focus on the dramatic moments, as if those times mattered more to Jesus. A closer examination of his life, however, leaves one with the impression that Jesus lived an utterly ordinary life, and from the ordinary he evoked the sacred—something so rare in his day (and ours) that Jesus was utterly extraordinary.

It was Jesus' posture toward the ordinary and toward the Mystery infused in the ordinary that gave him and his life such resonance. He knew that the presence of God suffused all moments, and therefore all moments contained this sacred dimension. He also realized that any division between the sacred and the mundane would block the vision and experience of meaning. So often he encountered people whose wonder for life was all but gone. He desired to re-ignite that wonder by reconnecting the sacred to the mundane. Consider this encounter.

> *1* There was a man of the Pharisee sect, Nicodemus, a prominent leader among the Jews. *2* Late one night he visited Jesus and said, "Rabbi, we all know you're a teacher straight from God. No one could do all the God-pointing, God-revealing acts you do if God weren't in on it." *3* Jesus said, "You're absolutely right. Take it from me: Unless a person is born from above, it's not possible to see what I'm pointing to—to God's kingdom." *4* "How can anyone," said Nicodemus, "be born who has already been born and grown up? You can't re-enter your mother's womb and be born again. What are you saying with this 'born-from-above' talk?" *5* Jesus said, "You're not listening. Let me say it again. Unless a person submits to this original creation—the 'wind hovering over the water' creation, the invisible moving the visible, a baptism into a new life—it's not possible to enter God's kingdom. *6* When you look at a baby, it's just that: a body you can look at and touch. But the person who takes shape within is formed by something you can't see and touch—the Spirit—and becomes a living spirit. *7* "So don't be so surprised when I tell you that you have to be 'born from above'—out of this world, so to speak. *8* You know well enough how the wind blows this way and that. You hear it rustling through the trees, but you have no idea where it comes from or where it's headed next. That's the way it is with everyone 'born from above' by the wind of God, the Spirit of God."[3]

Jesus longs to help Nicodemus connect to the sacredness of life in an ordinary conversation that occurs in the shadows of the night. Jesus uses all kinds of ordinary allusions to convey that a deeply sacred existence is not only possible but essential. From the birth of a baby to the dynamics at work in creation, Jesus revealed that the Spirit of the One is available and accessible to Nicodemus in everyday life. It is in the integration of life that comes from above and the one lived on the earth that we touch the sacredness Jesus portrayed to Nicodemus. A simple conversation, a miraculous revelation.

The conversation, the storytelling, and the very life of Jesus all pointed to this sacred connection and to his desire for others to experience it. He longed for people like Nicodemus and like you and me to touch the holy in the ordinary. This longing remains deep in the heart of every soul.

∿ Meaning in Activity ∿

Jesus showed us that all action, even routine action, contains a sacred dimension. The sacred is not just reserved for big events or religious contexts. The kingdom of God, or heaven, or whatever else you want to call this sacred dimension can be found here on earth as well, if it is not tainted with pride or power. This is what Jesus meant when he said, "On earth as it is in heaven." His prayer captured the yearning to express the Divine in the everyday, so that there would be no division between what we think of as heaven and what we think of as earth.

For too long, Christians have thought of heaven as a place where they will go when they die. Though Jesus spoke of something "more" after death, his preoccupation was with what was happening in the here and now. If Jesus could hear our concept of heaven as a place we go when we die, he might respond, "Don't wait until you die to go to heaven; go there now. Live from there now."

Humanity so needs this message. We need look no further than governments or religious or business institutions to see the abuse that has corrupted the sacred dimension. Business endeavors that have the potential to enhance the lives of millions can easily become little more than profiteering activities for a small, select group of misguided capitalists. Governments and religious institutions alike fall prey to a kind of unaccountable power that leads to manipulation, domination, and even abuse in the name of "the good," or worse, in the name of God.

We see the same abuse at play in our own hearts when we have lost connection with what is sacred. It is easy to distort the beauty of the present moment with selfishness and pride. Such distortions in our personal lives can ripple outward to distort our society and our world. Many of the woes we face locally and globally come as a result of a denial or distortion of the sacred dimension. Nations and groups of people harbor long-term hatred for each other because of a lack of connection to the sacred. This hatred leads to violence, and violence leads to war. The sacred is trampled on, and those bearing the image of God are killed in the name of God.

Images of this violence on the news baffle me. How can we treat each other with such disdain and contempt? But then I turn around and find contempt in my own heart. I dominate or manipulate my children in an attempt to ensure compliance. I find that the same dangerous dynamics at work in the nations of the world are at work in my heart. The seeds of profane living don't begin at the level of the nation but at the level of the individual. Change then begins individually as well, as we reconnect to the sacred and then allow that connection to move outward toward those around us. Humanity needs this connection and reconnection to the sacred. But how can we make it happen?

In his book *The Soul's Journey*, Alan Jones begins to explore this matter of creating heaven on earth:

We have to learn to be in two places at once: (1) grounded on the earth, accepting the limits of time, place and space as the gracious, non-punishing conditions of being human; and (2) defined by our destination in heaven, living into an identity that is open and formed by God. In short, to be human is to be embodied and engodded. We take our attachments seriously and refuse to let our exile keep us from our true destination. Yet what will happen next? And in our hearts the assurance: You haven't seen anything yet.[4]

Can you hear the echo of Jesus' words in Jones: "On earth as it is in heaven?" Being in these two places at once gives us the ability to notice and mine the sacred dimension in all our deeds. Heaven is a way of seeing life and a way of expressing what is seen.

The Eastern philosophy of Zen is helpful in its stress on and practice of finding meaning in the ordinary. Zen philosophy grew out of Buddhism. Though still rooted in Buddhism, Zen has taken on a life of its own. It is now often viewed as a "way" of living a life anchored in the present and appreciative of the ordinary. I remember listening to the Buddhist monk Thich Nhat Hanh speak several years ago (on tape) about Zen philosophy and the practice of presence, of finding the sacred in the ordinary. I found his ideas simple and even, well, boring. I heard him encouraging me to be present to my gait as I walked and to focus on my food as I ate it. Then he reminded me to feel my breath as it passed in and out of my body. There must be more, I thought. This man is a guru of sorts. And this is it? He wants me to pay attention to my food? My response at that time only revealed my misunderstanding of the nature of life. I was still looking for a magic idea that would help me escape ordinary life. Hahn was urging me to see the ordinary as the environment of the miraculous rather than an obstacle to it.

Hahn's advice is also found in the Christian tradition. Brother Lawrence, a monk from the Middle Ages, recorded his practice of God's presence and the sacred dimension of life through things like washing the dishes and doing the daily chores we all undertake. His counsel invites us to cultivate a kind of awareness that reminds us of Jones's idea: we are in two places at once, and we must allow each to inform the other. This awareness requires intentional practice if it is to become infused in our daily lives.

Over the years, I've attempted to cultivate this kind of attention to the sacred. I've discovered that this simple message is not as easy to practice as it sounds. It requires a kind of relaxed yet vigilant posture as I make my way through my day. The concept itself is not hard to comprehend, but the practice of it requires focused energy.

Many years ago, a friend and I tried to cultivate this practice through the changing of diapers. Yes, diapers. In a conversation, we wondered whether we could find anything sacred about changing diapers. Could God be present to baby wipes and diapers? Because we both had children in diapers at the time, we decided to put our questions to the test—to look for the sacred in the mundane, even the messy.

We were amazed to see just how sacred this moment could become. We began to pray and dream for our children as we changed their diapers. We became more aware of their bodies and their emerging personalities. We connected our own vulnerability to the frailty we saw in our children; we weren't so different from them. We too grew soiled in our souls and needed to be cleansed and refreshed. The realities and complexities of the day tarnished our souls, and we needed the Mystery's renewal on a regular basis.

The insights and intimacy grew with God as we connected the sacred to something often seen as a parental, necessary evil. I would encourage you to try this in your life. Choose a wholly ordinary task, and keep your awareness attuned to God—to the sacred—as you do it. You will be amazed at how the mundane becomes miraculous.

This cultivation of the sacred requires that I remove the obstacles (some of which I construct) that keep me from seeing what is in front of me. Though these obstacles can take many forms, at the core of all obstacles are two basic ideas. First, I block the sacred because I simply forget to notice that it is all around me; second, I lose touch because I've lost my sense of soul, my center. I dislocate from the sacred. Both obstacles are worthy of our attention.

∿ Forgetting to Notice ∿

It seems too basic to even mention, but one reason we are not present to the sacred is that we miss it as we make our way through the day. We say things like, "My heart just wasn't in it" or "I was on cruise control" or "I felt like a zombie." It seems odd, but true: we forget to bring ourselves into the action. Alan put it this way: "If there is action, real action taking place, then someone is doing the action. The trouble is that so often we are disconnected from the action, and then the action becomes meaningless."

When activity is separated from our hearts—the deepest part of our person—we become a shell of what we could be, and our action is less effective. This is what I had wondered at Starbucks before I went to meet with Alan. Were the people I saw (including myself) awake and attentive, or were they missing in action?

There are many reasons we forget ourselves in action. Routine can numb us, but we can also just check out and cease to pay attention to where we are and what we're doing. You can find an example of this kind of life-amnesia at your local grocery store.

Have you noticed just how lifeless a grocery line can be? Shoppers walk and talk their way through the store, but as soon as they hit the line, the life is sucked out of their bodies. They zone out or flip mindlessly through a magazine. Does even this description make you feel a little sleepy?

I like to mix it up in grocery lines, even though my family hates it when I do. Maybe they'd like to tell me, "Go back to sleep." But sometimes the forgetfulness in the line is just too thick, and I must do something, anything, to remind people that life exists, even in the grocery line. One afternoon, I was in my local store, standing in line. The checkout person, who must have been eighteen or nineteen years old, seemed to have a severe case of meaningless motion. It was painful to watch her scan my items. After she finished, I slid my debit card through the machine. She said, "It's processing; you'll have to wait a moment" (this is when my two sons headed for another aisle).

"Jill," I said, glancing at her nametag, "why do you think there's so much waiting in life? I mean, think about it, we wait to be born, to talk and walk, to go to school, to get married, and to advance in our careers." I took a quick breath. "We wait for our kids to be born, and then we wait for them to leave. Many of us even wait to die. What do you think all this waiting means?" By this point, Jill couldn't decide whether to answer me or call security. Finally, she did muster up the energy to ask me one question in return. "Do you want paper or plastic?" Meaning had once again been averted.

Jill and I had had an opportunity to remember that we were both living a life that holds so many questions—questions that reconnect us to the sacred. What could be more sacred than learning the powers that are at work in times of waiting? Yet to Jill, my question seemed odd and out of place. This wasn't the right moment to think sacred thoughts. You might think I just startled poor Jill, and she wasn't in the right frame of mind to deal with my question. To that I would say, "Exactly my point." The way we approach these everyday moments causes us to forget that we can be seekers at all times, not just when the moment seems right.

I often live just the way Jill does. I forget the treasures hidden in the normal. But still I long to excavate meaning out of more of these small moments. The routine parts of our lives seem tailor-made for this kind of sacred mining. But isn't it ironic? If I can't show up in a grocery line, where will I show up? It's as sacred a moment as any other, yet it is one that tends to be devalued. Maybe this is what Thich Nhat Hanh and Brother Lawrence meant. When we cheapen the need to be present to the simple, we will quickly forget ourselves and the Mystery in every other moment. If I can't find myself in a cup of coffee, I won't magically find myself when I turn to more important things.

∿ Becoming Dislocated ∿

There are other times we miss meaning in action, not because of forgetfulness but because of dislocation. We live in the past or in the future, not in the moment at hand, where the sacred dwells. Moments of dislocation are painful because we long to be present yet feel only the sting of the emptiness. And that is the dislocation of boredom.

Think about a time recently when you were bored. Try to describe the feelings that accompanied the boredom. Did you feel anxious, restless, or depressed? Boredom for me often manifests itself as a kind of antsy disappointment with the moment. How would you describe the feelings that came over you in the moment of boredom? What about your action? Were you satisfied with it? Did you feel a sense of fulfillment? Chances are, the answer to the last questions are a resounding no. We often think of boredom as a lack of significant activity. Instead, however, boredom is the dislocation of our essence in the midst of our activity that, in turn, leads to disconnection from the sacred. We might believe that the less we have to do, the more bored we grow. The truth is that the less connected our action is to the sacred, the more bored we become. Alan put it to me this way, "When you're bored, you're just not where the action is."

Perfect. You're also just not where the sacred is.

Because of our propensity to separate the mundane from the important, we attach boredom to the mundane and excitement to the important. From this view, much of life is mundane so much of it will also be boring. "I'm bored," may be best decoded as, "I've lost sight of the sacred in the mundane and am looking for something important that will enliven my senses." It's hard to deny that many of the choices we make when we're bored are our way of trying to spice things up. Unfortunately, the spices carry consequences. Diversion is the enemy of the sacred and the modus operandi of boredom. I do not mean to suggest that occasional breaks from work or rest and recreation are wrong. But diversion is destructive when we deliberately shift from one activity to another in the hope that the next activity will banish boredom. This is the root of many of our addictions. We are prone to addictive behavior to shield ourselves from boredom. Instead, we need a resolve to stay with the boredom until it leads us back to the present where the sacred awaits us.

Frequently, my boredom is attached to a disappointment I would rather not face. I feel the sting of a dashed hope and turn the disappointment over in my mind. I can obsess on why certain circumstance didn't materialize and how that makes me feel trapped. Soon I feel the energy drain out of me. I'm bored. Time for a distraction. This is when I'm prone to reach for a trinket that will end up in the graveyard. When instead I can stay with the feelings of disappointment and boredom, both lead me back to a place where real change is possible. I am able to face my over-inflated ego and the necessary limits that come with my humanity. I also find that I am more appreciative of what I've been given. Gratefulness seems to come as I face the boredom, not as I run from it.

Although boredom can trigger unhealthy activity, it is a wonderful and necessary internal indicator that we can learn to listen and respond to. What if we could reframe boredom as an early-warning indicator that we have lost touch with the sacred in the mundane? What if, instead of using boredom as a negative energy to propel us away from the mundane, we used its energy to propel us deeper into the mundane, deeper into the sacred and its meaning?

Let's go back to the story of my experience with the labyrinth at Grace Cathedral. In the experience itself, I was given the opportunity to connect with the sacred. However, I faced obstacles that had the potential to drain my energy and diminish my ability to sense the sacred. What I learned as I walked the labyrinth can help us as we walk the seeker's path day to day.

∿ Walking the Labyrinth ∿

My walk through the labyrinth before my visit with Alan would become, for me, a metaphor for my questions about the sacred mundane. When I entered the back of Grace Cathedral, I knew I would find a labyrinth. I was familiar with the work of Lauren Artress, a canon at the cathedral who has an intense passion to help people discover the transformative potency of the labyrinth. Feeling certain that these moments would be infused with the sacred, I knew this was a labyrinth I wanted to walk.

I was alone in the cathedral. Great, I thought. This is wonderful. No one else is here. I can share this moment with the Mystery by myself. Off came my shoes. I stood at the entrance and meditated quietly for a few moments. I lifted my foot to begin, and the moment seemed infused with the holy. My heart was reflective, and the space of the cathedral only added to the awe.

As my foot landed on the labyrinth, a noise distracted me. I ignored it. But the noise grew in intensity until I could no longer avoid it. Worse yet, in a matter of seconds, I realized the noise was coming from young children. Lots of them. Entire classes of children (row after row) now made their way into the cathedral for what appeared to be morning worship or chapel. From the very young to possibly fifth and sixth graders, here came lines and lines of children. Worse yet, many of them turned their heads in my direction and stared at me. Some giggled, and others sent me the message that I was interrupting them, not the reverse.

My heart sank. My sacred moment was over. I thought, I can't do this now. I can't believe this is happening. Why now, why today? And to top it off, I'm in my socks. Everything within me wanted to step off the labyrinth. Just step away. Don't begin. This is the wrong moment. Come back after the interview. This is embarrassing. And then I realized that this was exactly the right moment.

I had allowed the children to dislocate me from the moment at hand. Only seconds before their arrival, I was connected to the sacred. Yet when I believed the moment had lost its sacred quality, my thoughts and attention became distracted. Everything had been in its place for a great sacred moment, that is, until the mundane and intrusive presence of the children ruined things. I had created the perception that the moment was sacred because I was alone and felt connected to God. As morning chapel began, I lost touch with the sacred because I had narrowly defined what the occasion had to look like.

The real danger in all of this was the amnesia in my soul. As I had entered the cathedral that morning, I had an outstanding sense of the sacred. When the children came in, they shattered my hopes for the moment, and I forgot that I was still present to the sacred. Was this the fault of the children? Hardly. What could be more sacred than children? But my expectations were too narrow and easily dashed. To move beyond obstacles like forgetfulness and dislocation, it's important to keep our expectations of the moment pliable to avoid defining away the possibility of the sacred. I must absorb aspects of the moment that do not fit my expectations in order to evoke its sacred dimension. Seen in a different way, what appears to be the end of the sacred can simply be an invitation to go deeper into what is going on and find the sacred in the unexpected.

∿ Finding Meaning ∿

Early in our conversation, Alan and I talked about what we thought it meant to be a seeker. "Seekers" he said, "live in the rhythm of holding and letting go." This idea connects to this longing to move from activity to meaning. Part of the seeker's way is to discern, in the action, what we are to hold and what we are to release. There is no manual for this. It requires us to live awake and alert.

Too often, we hold on to expectations that diminish our ability to find the sacred in our action. Before I began my walk at the labyrinth, I expected that I would have the entire cathedral to myself. When my expectation was dashed, my sense of the sacred was clouded and my heart divided. Meaning seemed lost. To recover from this seeming loss, I had to let go of my insecurity and hold on to the conviction that this was the moment I was to walk. That moment now included the children. They would become part of the sacred, part of the meaning.

There was something else at work in me when the children entered the cathedral—embarrassment. It was one thing to walk the labyrinth alone. It was another to walk it in front of a hundred children. I had became afraid of what I would look like to them. The ironic thing here is the size of the cathedral. It's huge. There was plenty of space separating me from the kids. From my earlier description, you might think I was standing in their midst. I was not. But the fact that they could look back and see me made me afraid of being noticed. It got worse. A few minutes after the children entered, several other people entered the cathedral to look around. These people were just a few paces away from me. Once again I became distracted. This is really too much, I thought. I *can't* do this.

In the stories about Jesus and the people he encountered, Jesus often invited people to see the sacred dimension in the mundane. This required risk. The risk was at times attached to circumstances and other times to people. For instance, once when Jesus was passing through a crowd, a woman who had been ill with a bleeding disorder for many years touched his garment and was healed. Jesus stopped and asked who had touched him, because he could tell that sacred healing power had flowed out of him. The woman had to risk in that moment declaring that, in fact, she had touched him. She had no way to know what Jesus would do in response. Perhaps he would punish or embarrass her, yet the sacredness of that moment increased when she took the risk to speak up. The same is true for us. The sacred dimension is often evoked as we step out of our comfort zone.

∿ Putting It Together ∿

Perhaps all of this comes down to a new way to transform forgetfulness and dislocation into meaning in action. Consider this: *To find the sacred in the mundane is to locate ourselves (and the sacred) through re-membering.* By re-membering, I do not simply mean recalling—an activity of the mind. Rather, to re-member is to put ourselves back together in the moment of action. This relocates us and our ability to sense the sacred. What if Jill the grocery checker could have done this when I asked her about waiting? What if she could have *re*-membered that she and I are human beings capable of great reflection in ordinary moments?

Throughout this chapter, I've made a connection between finding the sacred dimension of a moment and finding ourselves—our essence or heart—in that same moment. The two are intertwined. We could say that when we find the sacred dimension we will find ourselves, and when we find ourselves, we will find the sacred dimension. When we are dislocated or forgetful in a moment, we become scattered and pulled apart. This is why we must re-member our lives in order to find meaning.

When I became embarrassed by the fact that there were children in the cathedral during my attempt to walk the labyrinth, I had to re-member myself if I were going to recapture the possibility of touching the sacred in that moment. All of the thoughts that assailed me in that moment were my ego's attempt to pull me apart and away from what mattered most. Because I chose to reconnect, meaning flowed. The walk revealed things to me about my own life and about my future calling. Most of all, it revealed what keeps me close to the sacred: my vulnerability.

∿ Returning to the Beginning ∿

What is a beginning point of practice for all we've discussed in this chapter? As I finished the labyrinth, it occurred to me how similar the labyrinth walk is to life. It would take an entire book to expound on these ideas, yet one idea is essential to this longing. The labyrinth reminded me that my mortal life has a beginning and an ending. Something about that stayed with me as I interviewed Alan. He tied it together for me when I asked him to describe ways he remains open to the sacred. He spoke of the need to remain close to his own mortality. In doing so, he said he is far more open to meaning because each moment is seen as a gift that will not last. Yes, I thought, just like my walk.

I was conscious of every turn of the labyrinth, because I knew each turn led me closer to an end, to a finality of sorts. I paid attention to what each turn had to show me and how I walked it because I could never get it back. This is the essence of *mortification*. Though the word has a bad reputation (for legitimate reasons), I believe the essential idea of it is tied to Alan's desire to remain in touch with his mortality. Mortification as a practice, then, is the ability to keep one's frailty in mind in each moment. In doing so, the vision of the mortal is more attuned to the sacred in all things.

Alan relayed a quote he had heard that crystallized this idea: "Live each day like it's your last, and one day you'll be right."

Beyond its humor, the quote beckons us to pay attention to each day because each day is a gift—a gift that, in its present form, will not last. Alan then quoted lines from Naomi Shihab Nye's poem "The Disappearing Act. "

> *Walk around feeling like a leaf.*
> *Know you could tumble any second.*
> *Then decide what to do with your time.*[5]

Beautiful. This is the practice of mortification at its best. It leads us to hold each moment sacred, not only because each one is sacred but because each one ends. When we recognize the fragility and transient nature of our lives, we tend to appreciate each moment we are given. The traditional sense of mortification was tied to bodily sacrifice or some sort of penance done to remember one's lowly position. But in its most basic sense, mortification comes when we remember that we are mortal, that we will die. From that place of vulnerability, we can learn to live our lives with a passion for each moment, because life is impermanent. Pride and denial can keep us from this way of living, as we maintain the illusion of our own invincibility. Perhaps this is why we are shocked when crisis visits our home or our community. We have simply removed the possibility of tragedy, so when it strikes we are aghast.

Nye's poem encourages us to live with our frailty in mind because it is from our weakness that we can most easily sense what is sacred. We can decide what to do with our days when we see them from a place of vulnerability, as opposed to a place of pride or selfish ambition. The Israelite King David reminded us of this posture through many of the psalms attributed to him in the Hebrew scriptures. No doubt David spent time outside, gazing at the night skies while he tended sheep or wondered what the day would bring. In these moments of feeling small (appropriately), David touched the sacred and wrote of his experience. His frailty led him to encounter the holy. It leads to ours as well. Consider Psalm 8. David begins by recognizing the limitlessness of God and the glory of nature.

> *God, brilliant Lord,*
> *yours is a household name.*
> *Nursing infants gurgle choruses about you;*
> *toddlers shout the songs*
> *That drown out enemy talk,*
> *and silence atheist babble.*
> *I look up at your macro-skies, dark and enormous,*
> *your handmade sky-jewelry,*
> *Moon and stars mounted in their settings.*
> *And this leads David to mortification:*

Then I look at my micro-self and wonder,
Why do you bother with us?
Why take a second look our way?[6]

This mortification leads David not to degradation of humanity but to recognition of humanity's place of honor.

Yet we've so narrowly missed being gods,
bright with Eden's dawn light.
You put us in charge of your handcrafted world,
repeated to us your Genesis-charge,
Made us lords of sheep and cattle,
even animals out in the wild,
Birds flying and fish swimming,
whales singing in the ocean deeps.
God, brilliant Lord,
your name echoes around the world.[7]

It was from this posture of mortification that David was able to sense both the sacredness of the moment and his own place in that sacred chain of being and events. David understood his frailty and decided to live a passionate life in light of that vulnerability. This is what connection to the sacred affords us: a healthy view of self and motivation to live every moment to the fullest.

NOTES

1. Kelly, T. *A Testament of Devotion.* New York: HarperCollins, 1941/1992, pp. 70–72.

2. Jones, A. *Soul Making: The Desert Way of Spirituality.* New York: HarperCollins, 1985, p. 4.

3. Peterson, E. *The Message.* Colorado Springs, Colo.: Navpress Publishing Group, 2002 (John 3:1–8).

4. Jones, A. *The Soul's Journey.* New York: HarperCollins, 1995, pp. 201–202.

5. Nye, N. S. *The Words Under the Words: Selected Poems.* Portland, Ore., Eighth Mountain Press, 1995, p. 29.

6. Peterson, 2002.

7. Peterson, 2002.

CHAPTER IV

From Control to Compost

Seekers: Phil Gulley and Jim Mulholland are Quaker pastors and authors. Together, in 2003, they wrote *If Grace Is True: Why God Will Save Every Person.* Both were authors prior to their collaboration. Phil is best known for his *Harmony* fiction series, and Jim wrote *Praying Like Jesus.* Both men are pastors and work with Quaker communities in Indiana.

I'm not a horticulturalist. I didn't grow up on a farm and learn to plant, wait, harvest, and celebrate the seed. I'm not sure why, then, I am so enamored with compost. We don't compost at my house, although we did talk about it once. I have seen an excellent example of compost at my friend Grant's house. That pretty much sums up my history with compost. I have no reason to be so captivated by it, yet there is something about compost that reminds me of, well, myself.

If I broaden my view of compost, I realize I'm a compost expert. Or maybe it would be better to say, *I am* compost. There are plenty of bits and pieces of garbage and bacteria in my heart. The circumstances and situations of my life often look like the shreds of paper, twigs, and leftover food that go into compost. Not to mention that I often feel like my life is in a state of decay. Upon closer examination, my bacteria, fungi, and decay seem to provide me with the conditions necessary for new and fertile life, just like compost.

We don't tend to view our lives as compost, but it's not a stretch to think this way. Author and futurist Len Sweet first introduced me to the compost-as-life-metaphor in his book *Soul Salsa:*

> A compost heap—this stewing, shredding, steaming, smelly cauldron of leaves, garbage, earthworms, insects, sawbugs, fungi and bacteria—is a thing of beauty. The gospel of grace is a waste aesthetic: there are treasure chests buried in trash cans. Grace moves us from buried trash to buried treasure.[1]

There are treasure chests buried in trash cans. What a wonderful way to view life. How often we hide our life-fungi and bacteria out of shame and embarrassment. The compost view of life brings us hope and the possibility of change. Imagine how this perspective could alter the way you deal with the various pieces of your compost. Instead of trying to hide or manage each element, we could allow the forces of the compost to turn those troubles into the raw materials of new life. Is it possible we've missed the inherent energy in the mess?

Recognizing the inherent value in mess is not a call to fill life with as much decay as possible. The infliction of excess pain is not the path to transformation. Nor do I, in any way, want to glorify the pain associated with trouble or the wounds that stem from dysfunction, dominance, and abuse. Neither is this a call for a soupy kind of emotionalism that dons a plastic smile when the harsh realities of life assail and disrupt. The trouble of life is trouble indeed. Yet a life-as-compost view teaches us that life is not to be managed and pain is not to be denied. Rather, all of life, including trouble, readies us for change.

When our dominant approach to life is one of managing rather than composting, we reduce life to an equation that must always balance out. This can produce a kind of rigidity that makes trying to control things our mode of operation. The compost metaphor invites us to relax our grip so that the forces of the compost—good, bad, and ugly—can work together to bring us to new places of growth and maturity. This movement from control to compost is the movement from human being as "manager" of life to human being as "participant" in life. Life is not meant to be controlled as much as experienced. But letting go of control requires us to move away from the kind of life we've grown to accept as normal.

∿ Getting Life Just So ∿

Much of life seems to be an attempt to get things just so, much like the arrangement of furniture in a room. We put the furniture just where we want it and expect it to stay there. The trouble with this view of our life-furniture is that it only works while we sleep.

For with the morning light come uncertainty, change, and instability. It's as if a nocturnal and divine jokester rearranged the furniture during the night. We're always startled by the rearrangements that life gives us because of that same old thing we've already talked about: we want a sure thing; we want answers that end the search. Our aversion to vulnerability leads us to create illusions of control. When we get the furniture of life arranged just so, we have at least something we can count on.

For many of us, "just so" takes the form of belief systems. The illusion that my belief system is altogether correct allows me a measure of control over my circumstances and over those who would seek to challenge me. Illusions of control can also take the form of politics, family, and possessions. Each can be used as a protective cover to keep uncertainty at bay and control possible.

The longing to move from control to compost teaches me to move from illusion to reality. This is a lifelong movement that we can never claim we've completed. To claim such a thing would only reveal how entrenched in illusion we remain. However, we do need some of our illusions; in any case, they can't be removed instantly. Imagine what would occur if we lost all our illusions at once. We'd go insane or become a mystic. Since the chances of complete and instant mystical transformation are low, it's more likely that we'll go crazy. So we don't even try to remove them but just think of life as a never-ending journey from illusion to reality. It is both a dynamic and emergent movement that requires us to embrace all aspects of life, both sorrow and joy, just the way a compost heap embraces everything that gets tossed into it.

The seeker's longing to move from control to compost comes as he appreciates life's events as fertilizer for the growth he desires. If our entire aim is to eliminate the mess and keep life contained and tidy and clean, we eliminate our ability to touch the Mystery, because we will seek to control the Divine just as we control the mundane. The Mystery is not controlled, only encountered and experienced.

Life, creativity, and wisdom flow out of forces like productive chaos and ambiguity. You may not think chaos can ever be something to embrace, but in fact it is. The ancient creation myth of Jews and Christians shows a kind of chaos at work in the formation of the universe. The text reads, "The earth was formless and void and the Spirit hovered over the deep." In this narrative, creation is not the result of high levels of control and measurement but arises from chaos that morphs into order, not once but again and again.

The creation story also reveals an important posture that the Spirit assumed during the creative and chaotic process. The Spirit hovered over and was present to the chaotic forces. The Spirit was not in a hurry to end the chaos but to work within it, to participate in and with those forces of chaos. This hovering over and within is the same posture you and I must assume in creating our life-compost. When we do so, we embrace chaos as part of the creative process rather than the enemy of the process. When we fight against the forces at work in our own decay, we are fighting against the very dynamic that brings us to transformation.

After I read Philip Gulley and Jim Mulholland's book *If Grace Is True,* I knew I wanted to dialogue with them about compost. When I told them this, they were unsure how to take the comment. Was it my subtle commentary on their book? We laughed. We laughed a lot that day. In fact, I found Phil and Jim to be among the most grounded and authentic human beings I've met. Full of humor and thoughtfulness, their love for God and compassion toward people are immediately evident.

I explained to Phil and Jim that, to me, their book is an excellent example of life-as-compost. The story of their journey to a new view of God's work in the world came out of the organic experiences of their life-compost. The book was less an expression of theological ideas and more one of a life journey that led both Phil and Jim to a different view of God, life, and salvation. This was a journey of the heart as much as of the head. Regardless of what one might think of the conclusions they have drawn, it is obvious that the process that brought forth the book came straight out of the compost heap. The genuineness of their personalities only confirms that they are making the movement from control to compost, changed by the forces at work in their particular heap.

Phil and Jim possess a rare blend of candor and grace. They are part of a small but growing breed of pastors who are willing to challenge the status quo of traditional evangelical Christian orthodoxy. The most recent manifestation of this challenge came in *If Grace Is True*. In the book, Gulley and Mulholland recount their journey of coming to believe that God will save all people. Their premise is this: eventually, no one will be outside God's grace or presence. This flies in the face of doctrines such as hell, predestination, and even, to some degree, free will. Phil and Jim explain their move away from a traditional view of salvation to a universalistic position in this way:

> Now I have a new formula. It too is simple and clear. It is the most compelling truth I've ever known. It is changing my life. It is changing how I talk about God. It is changing how I think about myself. It is changing how I treat other people. It brings me untold joy, peace, and hope. This truth is the best news I've ever heard, ever believed, and ever shared.
>
> *I believe God will save every person.*[2]

I knew I wanted to interview Gulley and Mulholland, not because of their views but because of the dynamics inherent in the journey they recount. It is a story of ambiguity, holy doubt, wondering, and challenge. These dynamics are all part of the seeker's way and the life-as-compost view, in which seekers hold their assumptions loosely and enter the process of change with flexibility and humility.

Jim and Phil are indeed seekers. As we sat on Phil's patio on a gorgeous September morning in Indiana, Jim explained that his mother had died when he was twenty-one. As Jim talked, the sound of a small waterfall in the background added a reflective tone to his words. The three of us waited a moment in silence as Jim's words sunk deeper in. Nature sang its song in the background through the chirps of birds and the sound of a gentle breeze moving through the patio. I sensed the sacred and felt that we were close to a tender place in Jim's heart. "When my Mom died, people gave me really pat answers about the tragedy that I knew just couldn't be true." Those easy answers that were given to Jim during this painful season of his life became a catalyst that turned him into a seeker. His seeker's heart has not only shaped him but has shaped the communities he has served and his work with them in keeping the questions alive and open.

Jim puts his desire to seek this way: "I don't do well in communities where there is no spiritual curiosity." Jim yearns to share his life with people who desire to seek beyond the obvious for the treasure hidden below. As he explained this, it occurred to me that Jim longed to be in a community where the compost was not simply at work in individuals but also within the entire community. I immediately pictured a group of people who became a communal compost heap and where the possibility of change was greater because of the collective wonder and curiosity of the group. I believe it's the kind of authentic community Jim described.

Jim relayed a story about a time in his ministry when he questioned his faith and beliefs. He shared his struggles with the people in his congregation. At one point, a woman spoke to him in nostalgic tones, asking him why he couldn't just "go back" to the way he was before all the questions had emerged. "Things were so good a few years ago. Can't you just go back to what you believed before all this searching began?" He told her he could not. This story seemed to be a defining moment in Jim's willingness to live life, not from a place of control but a place of curiosity and receptivity.

Phil shares Jim's desire to live in and out of the compost. As an author and pastor, he is committed to the quest of faith rather than safe boundaries and complete answers. Phil also understands the cost required to live in this manner—a cost that we must pay throughout our lives. He commented, "It's very painful to let go of things that once made wonderful sense, but through life experience we find out that those things no longer speak to our condition." This is the risk and the joy of the compost: it is a process of continual change.

In Jim and Phil's comments, I saw once again the importance of learning to hold and release our lives in a rhythm that allows for continual growth. To live in control is to deny the need for release. We obsessively hold onto ideas and things that were never meant to define us but to move us along through life. The longing contained in a compost view of life teaches us to travel the cycles of death (release) and new life (hold), putting everything into the mix and paying attention to all of it. Phil said, "For me it's an emerging sense that everything goes in the bucket instead of trying to separate what is sacred and what is not." If the longing to move from activity to meaning taught us that the sacred dimension is in all things, this longing helps us recognize that "all things" means even the pain and uncertainty of our lives.

Often the alternative to life-as-compost is life-as-an-object-to-control. This option is one we know all too well. Life-as-an-object-to-control allows me to have a fixed view of the world so that I can define, label, and judge each person and situation that comes my way. This control-based life will, for a while, create security. But that security is an illusion. We are a mess (a compost), and out of the mess, not separate from it, comes the possibility of new life. As I listened to Phil and Jim tell the story of writing *If Grace Is True,* it became evident that they were well aware of this embracing and engaging the mess—aware of its power and its peril.

∿ Embracing the Mess ∿

There's a paradox at work in the compost. On the one hand, we are invited to embrace a process that is bigger than us, one we cannot control but one to which we must surrender. On the other hand, the seeker's way calls us to actively participate in and shape what is emerging out of the readied soil. Though we surrender to the larger process, we are to engage this emerging life with passion. Herein we find another way to think about holding and releasing. We embrace the energy at work in the compost as something beyond our control. We cultivate the new life with as much care and intention as a farmer works the land.

This might be most true of my relationship with God. I cannot in any way control the Mystery or the experience of God. I can, however, live my life in ways that create receptivity to God's touch. I ready my heart as a farmer readies the soil, but I trust God for the life that will spring from that soil. I cannot make the growth happen. I can prepare the conditions that make the growth more likely. I work and surrender, and the dynamics in the compost fertilize the process.

Though we often do not understand what is occurring in the compost, it is essential that we stay with the process as it unfolds, even if it means that it takes us in directions we did not anticipate. Phil and Jim did not initially set out to write *If Grace Is True.* Rather, they were going to write a book on love, specifically, as love is described in I Corinthians 13. Phil said, "When we came to the phrase, 'Love never fails' we got stuck. We couldn't seem to move on or away from that idea. The more we sat with it, the more we knew the book was to be about something different." Their ability to hover in the chaos, in the "stuck" moment, created the fertile soil from which the book came.

Many of our woes come when we are not able to wait long enough for the chaos to yield its treasure. Our impatience kills the seeking. We need a different perspective on these moments. Here is one that has helped me relax and wait in times of ambiguity and uncertainty.

Imagine that your life is a series of approximations. At any given moment, the life you live is only an approximation of the life unfolding within you. In other words, the furniture in your life-room is never just so. Rather, you are always in the process of becoming. Can you think of a time you were quite certain you had life figured out, only to discover that the next season of life would undo that certainty? Why does this happen?

One reason for these ongoing revelations of our incompleteness is the fact that we are indeed always incomplete. We never arrive. Who I am now is transitory and only today's representation of a deeper person I am becoming. I've grown comfortable with saying, "I am living out my calling, approximately" or "I am the person I want to be, approximately." Who I am today is really me but not the final expression of who I will be. Ah, the compost view of life begins to take on even more appeal.

As we make our way through life, we recognize that today's approximation of life is tomorrow's decay.* The insights and growth of today will not sustain us for the long haul. We must let go of today's growth if we desire to reach new levels of growth tomorrow. However, the good news is that today's decay leads to tomorrow's approximation. It is often out of the staleness of life that we recog-

---

*I am indebted to Adrian van Kaam and Susan Muto for this idea.

nize our need for growth and are energized to enter the process anew. It's a day-to-day cycle of growth and decay, growth and decay, and growth. Through it, we move forward and grow deeper as human beings. This process yields the possibility of growth only as we wait on it and in it. If we shortcut the process, we shortcut life and end up living too long in today's approximation. To live in this sense of emergence requires us to embrace a continual kind of adaptation. We learn to move with this stewing, shredding, smelly chaos; the treasure is hidden within it and comes as we embrace and engage it.

Phil and Jim found themselves in the midst of the chaos—the compost—when their idea for a book didn't match what was happening in their hearts. Instead of ignoring the stewing and shredding, they embraced the swirling mess and waited for the life to emerge. Finally, the life came in the form of *If Grace Is True*.

Look back in your own life, and you will see this same type of composting at work. You could tell stories of times you thought you knew exactly where you were headed, but life moved you in another direction. The more you fought this movement, the more dissonance surfaced. But as you stayed with the mess, it led to the life. In fact, the more you embraced the chaos, the more fruitful was the creation of what emerged on the other side. This is the way of the seeker—to embrace and engage rather than control and confine.

The actual writing of *If Grace Is True* was a composting experience as well. Phil and Jim explained how they wrote the book. "Well, we played a lot of golf and talked a lot and wrote as well. The golf was really good compost." We laughed, and then Phil described how they work. "We spend a day a week together, and we write (or golf) during this time. But it's our entire relationship that becomes part of the process and the product." What a wonderful way to express it.

The seeker turns all of life into, well, compost. "Everything," as Phil said, "goes in the bucket." Imagine if you could see all of your life as a grand compost conspiracy. Everything in your life, from this view, is there to prepare you for successive harvests of life and meaning. It doesn't mean everything will be easy or fun. It means that everything works together in the compost. This helps us see that cooperation is at the heart of our human response to the Mystery's invitation.

Once the compost yields the beginnings of new life, then we do engage it with passion. When the sprout of life pokes out of the soil, it energizes us to cultivate the coming harvest. Phil and Jim found the energy needed to write their book once the composting process yielded the book they were to write. This point is important. To live in the compost does not mean we just wait around for the next season of chaos. When new life emerges, we must engage it. There is a difference between engagement and control. The dynamics at work in the process of composting teach us how to engage life without falling prey to either a rigid control or a flimsy passivity.

As Phil, Jim, and I talked, we saw the composting dynamic in two phases: (1) breakdown and conversion and (2) reformation and readiness. Each part of the process is critical to our experience of life and our ability to embrace and engage genuine growth. Let's explore each phase of the process.

Facing Breakdown

Life breaks down. This is a difficult concept to accept, much less embrace and engage. Things don't work the way we had hoped. As I approached forty, I noticed my body changing. I've noticed it's more difficult to read in dark places or without moving the print back and forth. This may sound small. And I thought it was small, too, until it happened to me.

I'm also looking my oldest son in the eyes when we stand. Both my teenage boys have realized that the day is approaching when they will be able to "take me." My only hope is they don't realize how close that day already is for them. Now when we wrestle, my body protests within thirty seconds. If they team up on me, it's not a pretty sight. My body is breaking down. Of course, my body is not the only area of my life that doesn't cooperate with my wishes. The list is actually quite long.

I often whine that life would be so much easier if things would go my way, since of course it is all about me. My plans and expectations are often different from the outcomes that follow. I'm frequently disappointed that my life doesn't seem to be moving at the speed or direction I had hoped it would. My agenda seems to break down on an almost daily basis. How about yours?

When life breaks down and I become vulnerable, that's when it's easy to move into control mode. If I try to control the changes or trouble spots, they seem to multiply. I experience the trouble of the moment and the trouble caused by my manipulation. Life then becomes a downward spiral of breakdown, disappointment, manipulation, and consequences. Then it all starts over again. Whether physical or not, breakdown is hard to face. No wonder we react by trying to control it.

In his book *For Everything a Season,* Phil told of watching his grandfather grow old and break down. It's a difficult and bewildering process. Phil wrote these sobering words toward the end of the reflection:

> There are times when I don't see him for several weeks. When I see him I am surprised at his decline. Were I to see him every day, I would not likely notice this slow breaking down. I am invariably alarmed and slightly panicked. Grandpa is fading, I think to myself. One day we'll come here and let ourselves in and he'll be lying in bed, drawn up and still.[3]

This is a difficult process to watch but one that is not reserved for the later years of life. The breakdown Phil wrote about is also part of each of our lives at a metaphorical level. Life breaks down and grows stale, and renewal becomes a necessity. This happens in situations, circumstances, and relationships. If we can realize that breakdown is a necessary part of renewal, we can bring to it something better than manipulation and disappointment. If we can see that without the breakdown of the garbage in the compost, we will not be readied for new life. We can relax in the times of decay, even see them as unlikely allies in our own maturity. Even physical death can be viewed as another breakdown that leads us on to a richer possibility on the other side. Rich possibilities are available now as well if we but learn to cooperate with the breakdown.

Losing Life

"Die before you die. This is the way we see it in the Muslim tradition."

An acquaintance of mine once shared this quote with a group of assembled leaders. The same idea is present in the Christian tradition. Jesus put it this way, "If you want to find your life, you must lose it." This wisdom reminds us that there is an appropriate kind of surrender necessary for life to flourish. When we hold too tightly to life, we block the emergence of the abundance we long to taste. It is when we face decay and breakdown that we need to embrace the wisdom of an early and metaphorical death. We must stop our struggle against the very thing that is a gift meant to move us forward.

To die to self is to die to the preoccupation with our own agenda and allow an agenda bigger than our own to prepare us for the next season of growth. We could all tell stories of a time that new life and new opportunity flooded into our lives only after we gave up trying to make it happen. These are examples of dying before we die. From that place of surrender and release, hope and possibility came to us. These times remind us and give us the courage we need to let go. The death I speak of is ongoing, something we face on an almost daily basis.

When compost is seen as a gift that helps us let go of that which has grown old, it becomes part of the way life and the Mystery prepare us for a richer experience. The trouble comes when we fight against these forces. This is a hard concept to embrace because we desire to rush on to new life. The compost teaches us that we cannot hurry decomposition. We must embrace it.

Phil and Jim wrote about the decomposition of their beliefs about heaven, hell, and judgment in *If Grace Is True*.

> I grew up believing we were destined for either heaven or hell. I was taught that only those who confessed their sins and accepted Jesus as the Savior before they died would live with God forever. As a child I never questioned this formula. It was simple and clear. As an adult, I'd held to this belief despite life's complexities.[4]

Life's complexities. This phrase is a good description of the forces at work in the compost that break us down. For Phil and Jim, the formula of their childhood no longer resonated with the experience of their lives. As this belief broke down, they were faced with a choice. Phil and Jim had to decide whether they would stay within the warmth of a belief they could no longer embrace or move deeper into the compost and risk the loss of status and security. This is a choice seekers make again and again throughout life.

Phil told me about the risk he had to take in writing *If Grace Is True*. "Things were going great with my book *Home to Harmony*. *Harmony* was selling very well and everything looked good for the future. Until, that is, we decided to write the grace book." When Phil told his publisher what he was planning to write, he was told that it would be the end of his contracts. "It was a very difficult time. . . . I had no financial security, and my wife had lost her job."

He paused and then continued: "What you learn in these moments is that control is fleeting. It's a lie that we can plan well enough and avoid all exigencies of life."

The breakdown phase of the compost challenges us to examine our cherished ideas and beliefs. Our view of the world, of God, of others, and of ourselves falls apart, and we are left to swirl about in the chaos of the moment. How tempting it is to revert to the safe or well-trodden paths of security and stability. We just need to get the furniture back in place and all will be well. Or so we think. But that is rarely possible. The breakdown shakes us at the very core of who we have been. Our old views seem hollow and unable to move us forward. We are in no-man's-land. The old no longer works, and the new has not yet emerged.

The in-between feeling I described is part of the reason we look for some measure of control. If in the decay we can find the courage to remain in the wasteland, a richer future has a chance to emerge. Phil had to let go of what had brought him security without the promise of new security. The question is whether we have the courage to stay within this breakdown time long enough for something better to spring forth. Often we find this courage, ironically, when we die to another cherished bit of security we have held so closely.

Facing Disillusion and Decay

Facing breakdown and decay can be disorienting. All that we thought worked no longer seems to work. Beliefs, ideas, and convictions no longer ring true. This moment is truly a dark night of the soul. We simply don't know what to do with ourselves or all that once brought meaning to our lives. We are disillusioned, and we think that is purely negative. We believe that if we could only go back, before the breakdown, to security and stability, all would be well.

Instead, what is needed is a new view of disillusionment. Disillusionment is not an enemy but a very important friend. The decay caused by life's complexities requires seekers to constantly reform beliefs that seemed etched in stone. Mystics are the best example of this. Mystics in every faith tradition have left behind a body of literature that reveals their willingness to let go of the known in order to embrace the unknown. They were willing to be disillusioned. Their disillusionment was the precursor to a vision that changed their world and in many cases changed the way millions of other people view the world.

The paradox here is that beliefs and life practices that once enlivened can grow stale and create rigidity, illusion, and blindness. Every so often, we need to be *dis*illusioned through breakdown. I've had many a concerned mother ask me to speak to one of her disillusioned kids. "I'm so concerned. He just started college and is so disillusioned with his faith. Can you talk to him?" It's at this point I normally say, "Well, to be *dis*illusioned is helpful, so don't panic. This is a good thing."

The conversation never goes over well. As parents, we are so conditioned to control that we never want to see our kids roam outside what we believe. If they are never disillusioned, they will fall into a sterile and empty faith, and for that matter, so will their parents. Phil, when speaking of the decay that led to his new view of salvation, put it this way, "What some people saw as an abandonment of truth became for me the embracing of a deeper truth."

The breaking down of life's illusions reforms our beliefs in a way that allows us to once again receive energy for the journey. Even if the breakdown leads us back to a reaffirmation of the same beliefs, the process is important because it makes our spirituality more authentic. This breakdown is far more than a shifting of our beliefs. It does something to us and in us.

Breakdown and disillusionment do something to my character and to my life. That something is conversion. The garbage, bits and pieces of stuff, and old dirt are converted—transformed—into something of value, something rich and ready. Much of this conversion is inward in this phase and outward in the next. Because of the conversion process, I become a different person.

Take, for example, the conversion in Jim and Phil's ideas about eternity.

> It's taken me years to empty my mind of hell. As a child, I was taught that only Christians will be saved. Billions of non-Christians would crowd hell. The thought of non-Christians in eternal torment didn't disturb me because I'd been told Christians were good people and non-Christians were bad people. . . . I remember the first time I seriously questioned this worldview. I was in college when I saw the movie *Gandhi*.[5]

The two authors then talked about their encounter with Gandhi and the authenticity they found in his life. One of them shared his admiration for Gandhi with a friend. The friend responded, "Isn't it sad that he's burning in hell?"

The authors chronicle the ongoing conversion of their beliefs that led them to a real change, not only theologically but in themselves: "The more patient I've become, the less easily I've assigned people to hell, the less I've wanted some to perish, and the more I've desired the repentance of everyone."[6]

Jim and Phil's beliefs did not remain lodged in their heads. The process of conversion does not allow for that. Their conversion changed their hearts and their actions in the world. Conversion makes us different in our sense of our place in the world, our ability to be kind, compassionate, firm, curious, gracious, and at peace.

The breakdown of the compost is not just a dirty trick of a vindictive deity or the random reality of a world without meaning. It is the way in which we are changed, converted, softened, firmed, and resolved. And it doesn't just happen once. It happens over and over. The seeker understands that this is an ever-deepening process and enters each new phase as if for the first time.

∿ Finding Readiness and Reformation ∿

The final phase of the compost is readiness. The day Jim, Phil, and I spoke, we also used the word *reformation*. I think both words are important to the concept. The process of breakdown and conversion reforms the heart and readies it for new life. Through this change, we are more ready to receive new life and new possibilities. We are also more eager to give what we have received to those around us. We long for others to taste the same fruit we've experienced. For Phil and Jim, this came in the form of an inward compassion and an outer conviction to share their view of God's grace for all people.

The process of breakdown and conversion readied Phil for a new life-opportunity he could never have made happen. The publisher of *If Grace Is True* decided to recontract with Phil to continue his *Harmony* series under their banner. Now Phil has a publisher who is interested in his emerging voice and grants him the space to continue the cultivation of that voice. He could not have orchestrated this himself if he had tried. The new life and opportunity came from the decay of the compost. Phil submitted to the process, which could not be hurried, and found that it led him to a place that fits with the person he is becoming. He put it this way:

> All of this was also very liberating. I used to think, what is the worst thing that could happen to me? My response

was, if I lost my contracts to write. And then I lost them. And something wonderful came out of it that I never anticipated. I now have a new publisher, and I'm free to really write what's in my heart. Life gave to me what I thought would be the worst and something wonderful happened. I'm free.

Reformation and readiness reignite our passion for life and allow us to express what we learned through the composting process. As we see the new life appear through the converted soil of our hearts and circumstances, a sense of gratitude overwhelms us. And we are emboldened to work with the compost process in other areas of our lives where we might still face decay. The more we can relax during the entire conversion process, the better. It may sound odd, but as we learn to cooperate with the compost and learn a new way of *being* compost ourselves, we come to experience the process as a grand adventure rather than as a necessary evil. The entire cycle excites us, because we know it is leading us to the next place of growth and transformation. It leads us deeper onto the seeker's path.

Think about yourself-as-compost for a moment. Can you see the new life that has come from past seasons of breakdown and conversion? It's important to re-member these times, because they give us hope and confidence to persevere in times of breakdown and conversion. If you come to a place in your composting where you are experiencing the pain of breakdown and conversion, don't give up. True, the lack of control and the pain can be overwhelming, but remember where the process is taking you: new life. Stay with your compost, and it will work its magic.

NOTES

1. Sweet, L. *Soul Salsa: Surprising Steps for Godly Living in the 21st Century.* Grand Rapids, Mich.: Zondervan, 2000, pp. 132–134.

2. Gulley, P., and Mulholland, J. *If Grace Is True: Why God Will Save Every Person.* New York: HarperCollins, 2003, pp. 7–8.

3. Gulley, P. *For Everything a Season.* New York: HarperCollins, 2001, p. 64.

4. Gulley and Mulholland, 2003, pp. 4–5.

5. Gulley and Mulholland, 2003, p. 162.

6. Gulley and Mulholland, 2003, p. 167.

CHAPTER V

From Shadow to Substance

Seeker: Lauren Winner is a graduate of Columbia University and Clare College, Cambridge. She has written for a number of publications, including *Christianity Today, Books & Culture,* and the Sunday *New York Times Book Review;* she has reviewed books for beliefnet.com. Winner has written three books, including *Girl Meets God,* which won her acclaim with a new generation of seekers who long to keep spirituality a genuine and relational endeavor. In it, she chronicles a period of her own spiritual journey in Judaism and Christianity.

In his book *The Great Divorce*, C. S. Lewis tells the story of a group of people who make a fictitious journey on a bus from purgatory to heaven. No one has to take the journey; anyone who wants to can stay in the "gray town" of purgatory. In fact, some people seem to make a life for themselves in purgatory and have little desire to leave. To these souls, purgatory is not such a bad place and even provides a measure of security. Others can't decide whether they want to leave or not. The security of what they know is hard to leave, but they are intrigued by the prospect of finding something new, something else. Still others appear ready to leave with the hope that something better awaits them—something that offers real hope for a way out of their colorless existence.

Eventually, a few curious travelers choose to take the bus and soon find themselves at the edge of heaven. Once at the outskirts, the main character in the story, along with others, makes his journey deeper into heaven. It is a journey that transforms the grayness of his soul into vibrant colors and deep textures. His journey is full of revelations about God, himself, and other people he meets along the way. Early in his journey, he makes a startling discovery about himself—one that shakes him at the core of his person. The discovery: he is barely real. He is more ghost than anything else. At one point he says:

> As I stood, recovering my breath with great gasps and looking down at the daisy, I noticed that I could see the grass not only between my feet but through them. I also was a phantom. Who will give me the words to express the terror of that discovery?[1]

As the character grapples with his own shadowy persona, he must face up to the fact that his condition stems from a lack of personal substance. There just isn't much about his soul that is authentic or lasting. His time spent in the world and in purgatory did not translate into a life of substance. Now, as he stands on the shore of heaven, he is faced with the reality of his situation. He is only a shadow of his potential. To make matters even more dire, this character soon discovers that not all the inhabitants of heaven share his transparent condition. In fact, some who call heaven home seem to be the very personification of words like *genuine* and *authentic*. These authentic beings, called "solid people," are described as "moving with order and determination" toward him and his comrades.

These solid beings become guides to the new arrivals and help them achieve a greater degree of authenticity, a greater degree of being. The book contains the story of this journey from shadow to substance and the many obstacles that seek to thwart the character's progress.

Lewis, through his description of transparent and solid people, describes what we all face as we make our way through life. There is within each of us a desire to become solid, full of substance, and authentic. Throughout life, we are plagued with the temptation to remain shallow and only a shadow of what we could become or what is possible. We might wonder why, but the truth is that it's easier to be shallow. As Lauren Winner put it in our interview, "There are many times my life doesn't resemble much of God's desires for me." Perhaps we can relate to her point that the current *expression* of who we are is not a good reflection of how we *really* are. What an odd but accurate thing to say.

The same idea is present in May Sarton's poem "Now I Become Myself." She muses,

Now I become myself. It's taken
Time, many years and places;
I have been dissolved and shaken,
Worn other people's faces.[2]

Sarton's poem describes the peculiar reality we face: we must become ourselves. And we must choose to do so. We can go through life without enough substance to move a piece of grass, let alone the hearts of those around us. Most of us do not desire such an existence, yet the alternative of authenticity comes with a set of challenges we find hard to embrace. To become myself, challenges and all, increases my authenticity. It is, in fact, the essence of authenticity.

∿ First and Second Authenticity ∿

I looked forward to my time with Lauren because I had just finished *Girl Meets God* and felt as though I knew her a bit. She informed me that we would need to start our meeting somewhat later so she could fulfill her obligations as a Sunday school teacher. Lauren was scheduled to teach the kindergarten class at her church and didn't want to leave the other teacher to the task all alone. I decided I would sit in. The restless ego in me was not happy about this change. Lauren's interview came at the end of a long week of travel, with more days ahead before I would be home. I wondered irritably why she couldn't just get a substitute as I made my way into the classroom.

Once in the classroom, I was greeted by a child trying to stand on his head. As I watched him, I was taken back to the wonderful early years of my own sons. When that led to the inevitable question of why they had to become teenagers, I laughed to myself and missed my family. As more children entered the room, the five-year-old's antics continued. Some laughed, while others showed me what they'd brought with them that day. Others tried to figure out what lesson or craft was on the dock for the morning.

As I continued to watch, it became serendipitously clear why my time with these children was essential to this longing and to my time with Lauren. These five-year-olds reminded me that we all make a journey away from and back to ourselves. That is the journey of authenticity. As we grow, we learn to hide and lose our original authenticity. This is not all bad. Without some inner partitions, life in this world would not work. But as adults, we tend to go overboard, adding to and shoring up these walls and adding steel supports to strengthen them further.

As I watched Lauren and her partner teach the kids that morning, I was struck by the fact that these kids were just beginning their journey to phoniness—to the partitions we know so well as adults. They were just old enough to begin the practice of deceiving, posturing, and hiding. It's an odd moment in life. They still had a measure of authenticity we adults often lack. Yet occasionally the cracks appeared, and out popped insincerity and disingenuousness.

As I write these words (at Starbucks, of course), there is, coincidentally, a little girl in the store with her mother. Perhaps two years old, she is still authentic. There is no guile in her, at least none I can sense. She simply is herself. If she wants to sing, she sings. If she wants to dance, she dances. Everything is grounded in *now*. She's not concerned about deadlines, money, bills, or what her friends think of her. But that will all come, won't it? Welcome to the world, little one. You are now solid. Soon you will learn to be shallow and make the journey back from whence you came.

Our First Authenticity

The authenticity of little children—what I will call *first authenticity*—can create awkward moments that remind us why we, as adults, choose phoniness. For instance, a professor at the seminary I attended had big ears—bigger than the average person's ears. There was no way to deny it. Even though we students all knew this, we weren't about to announce it at the next all-school gathering. Because he was a prominent school figure, there was an unspoken agreement to keep our opinions about his ears to ourselves. Someone forgot to tell my friend's three-year-old son about this agreement. When introduced to the professor, the first phrase out of the youngster's mouth was, "You have big ears." My friend was speechless with embarrassment. The professor handled it gracefully and agreed with the child.

At this point, my friend did what most of us would do as parents. He told his child that he had made an inappropriate comment: "We don't say that about others." It reminds me of my oldest son, who at the age of five went on a crusade to rid the world of cigarettes. When he saw anyone buying cigarettes, he would protest to us in loud tones. "Mom, that person is buying cigarettes. He is going to die." It only took a few of these outbursts for my son to learn that "we don't say that about others."

And that's how it goes. Our first authenticity is, well, too overpowering, too honest, and sometimes downright inappropriate. We learn to hide and shade our thoughts, words, and actions. We become phony, or at least divided. Don't misread this. I'm not advocating that we go back to our first authenticity. Rather, it's important to see some of the pressures at work in early childhood that influence our choice to hide ourselves. By the time we reach adulthood, it's possible to live so far removed from our essence that we are little more than a conglomeration of what we believe others want from us.

Our Second Authenticity

Most of our adult life is marked by the search for our second authenticity, which comes as we learn to be genuine without being inappropriate and authentic without grandstanding; we learn to live out of the person we are becoming rather than from the shadow of our substance.

The process of developing this second authenticity evokes the originality we tend to deny out of fear or compliance with the expectations of others. The second authenticity recaptures the wonder of the first authenticity without denying the reality of adulthood; it integrates the best of childlike simplicity with the wisdom we gain through years of life and experience, good and bad. The second authenticity enables us to live with candor and courage without abandoning gentleness and kindness. Most of all, the second authenticity allows us to find the unique person we are and honor our own unfolding, our own becoming.

In *Girl Meets God,* Lauren writes this:

> In the middle of my sophomore year of college, I dreamed about mermaids. In the dream, my friend Michelle and I and a group of women were kidnapped by a band of mermaids. They took us underwater, and though we didn't sprout tails or grow fins, we could function just fine on the bottom of the sea. We could breathe and walk around and talk. Life as a captive to the mermaids wasn't actually so bad. Our captors didn't keep us gagged or in chains. They let us do whatever we wanted, except go home. We could go to the movies, cook four-course dinners, read Ibsen. We just couldn't return to the shore.[3]

Lauren then describes her rescue.

> After a year underwater, a group of men came on a rescue mission. Most were gratifying, paunchy, fifty-something men, Monday-night-football-watching types. But one was this beautiful, thirtyish, dark Daniel-Day-Lewis-like man. And I knew that he had come to rescue me. He would, of course, participate in the group effort while he was there, but I was the reason he'd come.[4]

Later in the chapter, Lauren relayed that she believed the man in her dream—the one who had come to rescue her—was Jesus. That belief became a defining icon in her faith and journey toward Christianity. I have an additional interpretation of the dream—one that I'm not sure Lauren would agree with. I discovered the story after our interview and decided not to ask. I believe, nonetheless, that the home the mermaids will not allow her to return to is her heart, her true self, her essence, and the gift of God that longs to be discovered in her.

Lauren's dream could be seen as an archetype of sorts for the journey to the second authenticity. We've all been kidnapped. The cause of the abduction varies according to the story of one's faith tradition. Most traditions agree that we are lured away from ourselves and persuaded to forgo the journey home, to God, and to ourselves. We can do anything else we would like as long as we don't go home. Don't take the bus to heaven; stay trapped in lesser things.

Girl Meets God is a story of homecoming, although it's a homecoming in progress. She wrote it in her early twenties. There's more "becoming" ahead for her, as for all of us. However, to view life as a story of homecoming is both important and energizing, as long as we remember that we never fully arrive home. The journey is ongoing, the story always unfolding. To see life as a story full of characters, plots, and drama has tremendous merit. When we read our lives in this fashion, it's easier to sense the dynamic unfolding, with its twists and turns. We can more easily view ourselves as unfinished characters in search of authenticity.

The opposite of the unfolding-story view of life is the static view, which places each person in a box, permanently. This can be a political, social, or religious box, to name a few possibilities. But it leaves us wanting and longing for something more, something authentic. The more we box others in, the more evident it becomes that we long ago boxed ourselves in. This creates the very narrow view of life that this book seeks to enlarge. C. S. Lewis describes this narrowing view of life in *The Great Divorce*. The main character experienced the rigidity of purgatory in the following manner:

> They've got cinemas and fish and chip shops and advertisements and all sorts of things they want. The appalling lack of intellectual life doesn't worry them. I realized as soon as I got here that there'd been a mistake. I ought to have taken the first bus out but I've fooled about tying to wake people up here. I found a few fellows I'd known before and tried to form a little circle, but they all seem to have sunk to the level of their surroundings.[5]

Lauren wrote of a similar woe she experienced with certain friends who want to contain her life at the level of their own.

> Evangelical friends of mine are always trying to trim the corners and smooth the edges of what they call My Witness in order to shove it into a tidy, born-again conversion narrative. My story doesn't fit well with this conversion archetype. A little scholar would say there are too many "ruptures" in the "narrative." But she might also say that ruptures are the most interesting part of any text, that in the ruptures we learn something new.[6]

I would add that we *become* something new, something of ourselves. We all bristle when we are defined with such narrow tones. When people want to shove our lives into a box, we react because we know deep down that we are more than the label implies. We also bristle at the disregard for the reality that we are becoming more than we are in any given moment. As Kierkegaard said, "Label me and you negate me."[7]

The second authenticity makes us "solid people" in the way C. S. Lewis used the expression. The seeker's desire is to make this journey home, with the help of the One who yearns for people to come home, to find their essence in relationship to the Mystery. Homecomings unite the self and the Mystery in a natural and intimate relationship that each is longing for. Though this journey is a challenge, the seeker looks to make it each and every day. We can press through the challenges of this journey as we live in and out of two significant choices. First, every day we choose our essence over a more surface image. And second, we choose brokenness over perfection.

∿ The Choice of Essence Over Image ∿

The journey to second authenticity is a choice of essence as opposed to more fleeting appearances. As I write these words, I am sitting in the food court of a mall in the city in which I live. It becomes clear, as I watch people pass by, that for many, appearance is essential. Maybe a better word to use is *image*. We are all interested in our appearance to some extent. We want our hair to be combed and our bodies and personas to be as well kept as possible. This is not a bad thing. In fact, moving beyond basic hygiene, it's not wrong to see clothes and demeanor as a way of revealing our original self. However, this idea can easily move from healthy expression to unhealthy obsession. Healthy outward expression is not far removed from a place where there is little to us beyond the image we seek to display to the world. When we spend too much time making statements about our importance based on the clothes we wear, our hairstyles, and even our walk, we have little time left to cultivate a deeper and more substantial self.

The trouble with an image is that it does not guarantee that the one behind it is a genuine article. Image can be more for show than for anything else. This idea is easily seen in the current cultural phenomenon known as "American Idol." This reality TV show seeks to find the best singer in the country, according to a panel of three experts and eventually the viewing audience; the experts and the audience vote. At the writing of this chapter, the show is in its third season. I had never watched it until this season, when my family and I decided to follow the entire season, from beginning to winner. As we watched the early weeks of the show, I was amazed at how many "singers" were driven by an image of their favorite singing star. Many contestants were simply playing a part they hoped would get them noticed. Instead, it usually got them disqualified.

Early in the season, singer after singer stood in front of the three judges to display their voice and "talent," in hopes of making it to the next round. For the most part, the singers were, well, in need of a dose of reality. Most couldn't sing. There was absolutely no substance behind the image they projected. What's worse, many seemed to have taken on the persona of a famous singer and showed no trace of their own originality. From dress to movement, those nonsingers played parts that bore little-to-no resemblance to themselves. It was obvious by their awkward action that the personas didn't fit, weren't genuine. They may have looked the part of a pop idol, but their appearance was all image; little substance backed it up. And it was sad to see how many believed in the image they portrayed. They believed those mermaids who kidnapped them and told them they could sing all they'd like; they just couldn't go home. It is as if they had looked at their image for so long that they couldn't see anything *but* that image—one that didn't reflect their unique and authentic gifts.

As I was shaking my head in disbelief at the show, I remembered that I, too, fall prey to this woe. How easy it is for me to portray a persona that I believe will enable me to get what I want. I let an outer shell influence me until I believe the shell *is* the substance.

Writer and teacher John Eldredge calls the desire to flaunt image for gain "posing." In an attempt to prop up our weak egos, we try to look the part, posing for the camera and the crowds.

In the New Testament, we read of a group of posers who were all about image. They were actually the religious leaders of the day, like your neighborhood pastors and priests. These religious leaders were driven by a religious and moralistic persona. They looked the part of holy men who were spiritually connected to God, but in reality, as Jesus seemed to love to point out, they were full of decay on the inside. They chose image over essence, and it created a desire within them to keep others from making the journey to second authenticity. The words of Jesus in the gospel of Matthew reveal the image-over-essence life of these leaders.

> Woe to you teachers of the law and Pharisees, you hyp-
> ocrites! You are like whitewashed tombs, which look good
> on the outside but on the inside are full of dead men's bones
> and everything unclean. In the same way, on the outside
> you appear to people as righteous but on the inside you are
> full of hypocrisy and wickedness.[8]

Jesus lived the opposite of an image-driven life. What attracted people to Jesus was not only his originality but his ability to evoke that same second authenticity in the hearts of those around him. His life was a threat to the narrow and rigid and a breath of fresh hope to the oppressed and downtrodden. Jesus was a threat to many religious leaders because he exposed the persona that kept them in control of the compliant. He enabled the weak and vulnerable to know their originality as they touched the Mystery. Jesus revealed that to find one's own originality is to find the presence of God—the Mystery—in an immediate and transformative way.

Jesus put it this way: "Love the Lord your God with all your heart, soul, mind, body and strength. And love your neighbor as yourself."[9] Marcus Borg, whom we will meet in the next chapter, calls these the two great relationships. In other words, each relationship enables the other to flourish. We find ourselves as we find the Mystery at work and play in our daily lives. We find the Mystery as we live authentically and help others do the same. This dynamic relational flow keeps us connected to our essence rather than driven by an unanchored image.

The path of the seeker follows a trail away from image and toward essence to know the self that is emerging within, to take time to find this inner self and let it influence the body and the persona. We are all tempted to live in a persona that isn't real but conveys an image of power or beauty or whatever we deem important. Often those around us can spot the phoniness of the image long before we can. Instead of a persona pushing its way to the center, life is about allowing our heart to push itself out from the inside.

This lifelong process is often painful. But it is often out of that pain that the authenticity we seek has the opportunity to surface. This pain can occur at any time but seems prominent in our adult years. As children, we are invited to grow up. As adults, the invitation is to grow out of these personas as we embrace the frailties and beauties of our personalities, quirks, bright spots, and dysfunctions. Brokenness has a way of giving us the courage we need to shun the persona and embrace our truer self, warts and all.

∿ The Choice of ∿
Brokenness Over Perfection

Our first authenticity is lost over brokenness. We get hurt and wounded in life and lose our childhood innocence. Our second authenticity, ironically, is found through brokenness. Brokenness plays an interesting role in our lives. Though the age is different for all of us, at some point in childhood or early adulthood we realize that the world is not as we once thought. Adam and Eve's banishment from Eden in the book of Genesis is a story that happens to all of us.

At some point in my twenties, my life fell apart. To the casual onlooker I'm sure I seemed fine, but I was adrift in a sea of doubt and disbelief. My life had been a series of steps on firm ground. I was confident in myself and my image. Then I stepped on a rock that wasn't secure, and the fall broke me open. Until that moment, I had always thought the ground below me was padded, in case of just such a slip. But it wasn't. When I hit, I expected the ground to break my fall. It didn't. I lost my way and my faith. I wasn't even sure I believed in God, which is an occupational hazard for a pastor, my vocation at the time.

The outer details of my crisis aren't all that important to this story. In fact, the specifics aren't impressive at all. I'm confident that most of humanity experiences far greater pain than I experienced during that season. What is critical is the utter inner ambiguity that ensued. I was lost. Part of my extreme undoing came because of what my brokenness revealed. Far more than a wound, my brokenness was a mirror that reflected something back to me that I had not expected. I wasn't a solid person. There wasn't much to me. Although I had appeared solid for many years, it was more image than essence. As a result, I did not posses many inner resources to draw on in order to heal and grow. Looking back, I see that this brokenness was critical to finding a more genuine path. This has been true of brokenness in my life since that day.

Our second authenticity—becoming ourselves again—comes when we realize we've been too long in the land of the mermaids. It's painful because, like the loss of our first authenticity, the second is initiated when we see that the life we've lived must end. We must grow up—again. This maturation process is psychological, emotional, and spiritual in nature. Much of what we come to discover through our banishment from Eden is how little we know about ourselves and the Mystery. The hope of the second authenticity is that these relationships can be cultivated and that pain is not a cosmic joke but part of what makes us more genuine people.

The obstacle we must overcome in brokenness is our propensity toward perfection. By perfection, I do not mean error-free living. Most of us can handle the little gaffes of everyday life. What is harder to handle is a tarnished image. When we are exposed as frail, it is altogether different. Even though we know, in an abstract way, that everybody is frail, in between the first and second authenticity we spend a lot of energy proving our image is untarnished (or tarnished in ways that don't matter).

Brokenness, in the first authenticity, pulls the covers off life and reveals to us that people and situations aren't perfect. People and situations aren't what they seem to be and, in fact, can hurt you. If only we could also learn that we are not what we seem either and must enter a process of healing and restoration. For most, that's too much to bear as we lose our first authenticity. Many of us discover this first brokenness in our early years of adulthood when it's easier to blame than to reflect. We instead learn to protect ourselves from those "out there" who would do us harm. All along, we let the most subtle of saboteurs stay put. Brokenness initiates the second authenticity because it often exposes the saboteur in us.

In the crisis I described in my late twenties, it was easy, early on, to blame everyone around me for my plight. It was my church's fault, or maybe my religious tradition in general, or perhaps my family, or the circumstances I faced. It was much harder to face the truth that I had contributed to my own demise. I had not cultivated a life of substance but lived on the surface of my connections to people and the adulation I could receive from a job well done. It was through the gentle patience of a Jesuit spiritual director that I was able to face the hollowness of my persona and the adventure of discovering the authentic "me" who was yearning to be found and expressed.

All this sounds harsh. I do not mean it to be at all. Brokenness, in both the first and second authenticities, is a gift of great value. We can't live in the Eden of our childhood. Neither is the disingenuousness of our lives a good lifelong condition. Brokenness is a gift that moves us along. Each broken season of life presents the possibility of more authenticity and substance. It's like that composting process we discussed in the last chapter. The pain and difficulty of life is often the pathway to real change and authenticity.

Living Authenticity
Through Spiritual Friendship

The cultivation of authenticity cannot be accomplished alone. Without the friendships of others, we are lost in our attempts to prop up images that will never satisfy the deeper longings of our heart. We need each other if we are to make the journey. Friendships can be a wonderful part of our journey, but they can be hard to embrace. In the first authenticity, we discover that some people are not as they appear and that we are vulnerable to pain. This creates a distrust that can hinder our ability to enter intimate friendships where healing and growth can occur.

The good news is that in the journey toward our second authenticity, we find that relational pain does not have to be the final story. We find others like us who are broken and are searching for greater originality. These people become guides, wounded healers, and friends who walk alongside to encourage and support us. We do the same in return. In *The Great Divorce,* Lewis's main character had a guide who walked alongside to help point out the way and impart wisdom. It is critical to the second authenticity that we find these safe yet challenging friends who will walk with us.

When I read Lauren's memoir, I was struck by her relationships and how formative those relationships were to her experience. Even though the book detailed a part of her personal journey, it did so with the company of many others who were also on the path of the second authenticity. Her friends challenged, questioned, and encouraged her along the way. They pointed out to her times when she abandoned her second authenticity and celebrated with her when her originality emerged.

Lauren put it to me this way: "Friends 'authenticate' us insofar as they remind us who we are and why we do the things we do." It's as if our friends tell us when we are or are not being true to our second authenticity. This is how I take Lauren's word *authenticate.* I like the idea very much. Though we can never fully rely on (nor should we) the view of friends, their view is important nonetheless. They help keep us true to the life that is unfolding within us, and they challenge us to make sure our attitudes and actions align with that emergent life. Yes, they authenticate us.

In his book *The Genesee Diary,* Henri Nouwen makes this statement: "The way to 'God alone' is seldom traveled alone."[10] In other words, when God is at the center, it in no way diminishes the importance of friendship and community. To know God means to discover him in relationship with other people. In doing so, we find ourselves moving closer to each other and ultimately closer to God. This brings us back to the story of the Good Samaritan that we touched on in Chapter Two. A deeper look at the story reveals three gifts spiritual friends give each other as they walk the seeker's way: seeing, feeling, and acting.

Seeing, Feeling, and Acting

The story of the Samaritan's gift to the wounded man begins with the man being seen. Whereas the other two passersby refused to register the traveler's pain, the Samaritan "saw" his wounded condition. We cannot help each other move toward a more authentic expression until we are fully aware of the other person.

How often I've missed the condition of a friend because I didn't pay attention to the clues that were right before my eyes. I missed the wounds, the pain standing in front of me. Or worse yet, I simply ignored a friend's wounds, just as did those who walked on by in the New Testament story.

When we are consumed by our own agendas and activities, it's almost impossible to see the hurt and brokenness around us. Without a change of perspective, we'll never be able to help anyone. Spiritual friendship begins with awareness. Until we notice others' pain, we can't help them. But vision alone is not enough. The religious people in the Good Samaritan story noticed the man but still chose not to intervene. They did not have the deep feeling that led the Samaritan to offer help. The Samaritan took pity on the man left beaten on the side of the road, because he had suffered his own wounds as part of an outcast group in that place and time. Samaritans were considered half-breeds in their day—not fully Jewish, not fully gentile. They were ostracized on both sides of the cultural fence. This man, therefore, knew the pain of rejection and the sting of wounds inflicted by those with more power. Surely, the Samaritan's own pain and brokenness enabled him to move toward rather than away from the man on the side of the road. This is true friendship—friendship that springs from our second authenticity. The religious leaders who passed by felt no common feeling for the suffering of the wounded man—feeling that would have made them more likely to help him.

Compassion—the ability to connect your own pain to the pain of another—is another word we could use here for deep feeling. Compassion isn't just feeling bad for another person. It means feeling your own wounds again as a way of becoming vulnerable to the pain of the other person. Until we connect ourselves to the pain and frailty of another, we can't really help him or her. When I view people as an inconvenience, I'm doomed to walk right by them because I'm just too important for my own good. Spiritual friendship emerges as we can live our brokenness out in front of each other. From that brokenness, we can help to heal the wounds of a friend.

I have a friend named Mike. I've known Mike for eleven years. The first time we met, we hit it off. Our personalities seemed to quickly mesh, and our humor was and is complementary (often to the chagrin of our wives and mutual friends). There's far more to our friendship than fun and games, though. Mike and I are spiritual friends who help each other find and follow the second authenticity through the wounds we've experienced.

For over eleven years, Mike and I have listened to each other share our wounds, frailties, and dysfunctions (as well as our dreams and victories). We have listened to each other, cried, and occasionally even laughed about the brokenness we each possess. What has made my relationship with Mike so powerful is the absolute honesty we give each other about our flaws and frailties. We don't try and prop up an image in front of the other that is flattering (well, we sometimes do try to this, but the other quickly recognizes it). We simply are who we are, and we help each other become more than what we are at the moment.

I know Mike is human and wounded, and he knows the same about me. This has created a safe place for us to grow and explore our lives. I am confident that without this raw honesty, our friendship would never have become the haven it is. The irony is that out of the pain of our composted lives we can offer each other space to grow in authenticity. What a gift indeed. It sounds odd to say, but I'm glad for our frailties and wounds because it is through those painful places that we offer each other a friendship that leads to healing and vitality.

Vision and deep feeling are essential for spiritual friendship, yet heart-felt compassion must translate itself into concrete words and deeds. The Samaritan, at great cost to himself, brought aid to the wounded man. He laid his own resources on the line. If we are to help each other make the journey toward a more authentic self, we must turn our compassion into tangible expressions of service. The circle of friendship isn't complete until it manifests itself in action.

Seekers are not meant to travel alone. We will revisit this idea in another chapter, but it's critical to understand it when we think about movement from shadow to substance—a journey we cannot make by ourselves. Too many snares line the path; self-deception, discouragement, distraction, and pain thwart the seeker's desire. Second-authenticity friendships enable us to keep going and remain honest as we go. It is easy to fall back into our own phony devices that convince us to go back to where we're more comfortable. The journey to the authentic self and the Mystery that makes it possible is long and, at times, arduous. We need each other.

You may be leery about letting another person into your brokenness, into your lack of authenticity. This is understandable, and we must be wise in our choice of second-authenticity friendships. I have found that these friendships emerge over time. It is unlikely you will dive into second-authenticity issues the first time you meet someone, although people who are spiritually and psychologically attuned to the Mystery can close the gap quite fast. And there are the rare gifts of people we seem to resonate with from Day One. Most friendships take time and require a trust that is not earned overnight.

Second-authenticity friends are not around to keep you on the straight and narrow in parent-like fashion. They walk beside you, and you beside them. They see, feel, and act in ways that support your transformation. You do the same in return. Together, you encounter zones of brokenness and the shadows that lie behind that brokenness. The joy of friendship is that you can help each other find the more authentic you that hides behind the pain and is waiting to be born into the moment. You help each other *become.*

NOTES

1. Lewis, C. S. *The Great Divorce.* New York: Collier Books, 1946, p. 28.

2. Sarton, M. "Now I Become Myself." In *Collected Poems, 1930–1973.* New York: Norton, 1974, p. 156.

3. Winner, L. *Girl Meets God.* Chapel Hill, N.C.: Algonquin Books, 2002, p. 55.

4. Winner, 2002, p. 55.

5. Lewis, 1946, p. 14.

6. Winner, 2002, p. 7.

7. Attributed to Kierkegaard.

8. *The Holy Bible: New International Version.* Nashville, Tenn.: Broadman & Holman, 1986 (Matthew 23:27–28).

9. *The Holy Bible: New International Version,* 1986 (Matthew 22:37–39).

10. Nouwen, H. *The Genesee Diary.* New York: Image, 1989, p. 11.

CHAPTER VI

From Performance
to Expression

Seeker: Marcus Borg is the Hundere Distinguished Professor of Religion and Culture at Oregon State University. He has written numerous books on a variety of Christian and spiritual themes, including the Bible, our images of God, and the life of Jesus. His books have been translated into seven languages, and he lectures extensively in North America and overseas. His most recent book, *The Heart of Christianity,* helps to reframe Christianity for those who desire a faith that can speak to the realities of life in the twenty-first century.

In 1989, the wildly successful movie *Field of Dreams* touched a longing for authentic expression. The movie is set on an Iowa farm and wrapped around Ray Kinsella's love of baseball. Ray is married to his college sweetheart, has a young daughter, and drives a Volkswagen bus. As the story opens, you get the feeling that Ray's life is flat, going nowhere.

Soon Ray hears voices in his cornfields, and things get weird. The voices tell him to build a baseball diamond right out in the cornfields—to build a field of dreams. One by one, famous baseball players from the past mysteriously make their way to the field and relive their days as players. Ray lives his dream of watching them play.

This story has many subplots. One occurs well into the movie, after the field is built. Ray takes a trip to enlist the help of Terrence Mann—a famous writer and icon of the sixties. Ray convinces Mann to come to Iowa and experience the field of dreams for himself. On the trip back to Iowa, the two men pick up a young hitchhiker who happens to be a baseball player from an earlier era named Moonlight Graham. Graham, when alive, had played only half an inning in the major leagues before he left the game to study medicine. He never got a chance to bat or, as he put it, "to stare down a major league pitcher just as he goes into wind up and wink at him to make him wonder if you know something he doesn't."

One of the last scenes in the movie shows Ray arguing with his brother-in-law, who is the voice of convention and rigidity. He tries to convince Ray to sell the farm because Ray is broke. Ray and his brother-in-law get into a tussle, and Ray's daughter ends up on the ground. The impact of the fall causes her to begin choking on a piece of hotdog.

With his daughter choking, Ray looks at Moonlight, who he knows can save his daughter. Moonlight runs up to the line dividing the field from the stands. He stops and realizes the choice before him. If he steps off the field, it will end his dream. He will return to the condition in which Ray first encountered him. He decides to cross the line and save Ray's daughter. When he does, Graham is transformed back into an old man. Moonlight is at peace with his decision to step off the field because he knows his life as a doctor represents the deeper expression of his life. Though he wanted to perform at the plate, in the end he traded that moment-of-glory performance in order to express his calling as a physician.

Every day we face decisions similar to Moonlight Graham's. Will we express what is original and important to us? The more authentic we become, the more we want to express the desires of our heart. Like an artist who seeks to express the art inside her on the canvas or through another medium, we long to express our life on the canvas of the everyday. We want to leave our mark on the world. That mark begins as a stirring inside us that must be expressed. Beethoven had to express himself musically, Van Gogh through painting. Though our medium may not be music or painting, we too feel the need to express the life we feel inside—another unavoidable dynamic of being human.

It is not, however, a foregone conclusion that we will express this original self we sense inside. Lesser expressions lurk close by. We can settle for a kind of activity that draws us away from what matters most to us, away from our second authenticity. The seeker's way is lined with the choices between momentary performance and lasting expression. We can waste our lives on trifles that provide temporary satisfaction but lead us back to the graveyard. We can spend our time on activity that props up the personas we examined in the last chapter. This happens when we buy the lie that power, material possessions, amusements, or status is the reason for our existence. When we have those motivations, we choose activity that increases the lie. Unfortunately, when we run after lesser things, we have little time left to discover the real purpose for our life and how to express it in the world around us.

∿ Performance-Driven Living ∿

Performance, for our purposes here, is defined as action that betrays or retards our second authenticity. It disconnects my inner self from my outer action. I am not thinking here of performance in terms of a singer who performs for an audience or an athlete for a prize. Performance for our discussion is action that is motivated by the ego's desire to inflate the self's importance and live on the fumes of aggrandizement and ambition. Moonlight Graham chose to let go of action that would only bring temporary affirmation so that he could act in a way closer to his second authenticity. He made a choice to step across a line. The same choice awaits us.

Dysfunctional performance originates from two places. First, we feel an unhealthy pressure to perform in any given moment. Whether because of internal pressure or because of others' expectations, the desire to get life perfect can be intense. The stress of it all can seize our emotions and wreak havoc on our bodies. Millions of dollars are spent each year on medications and medical procedures for treating unhealthy levels of stress that rob us of joy and deplete our energy.

A secondary but powerful source of unhealthy, performance-driven living comes from the vestiges of our childhoods. We are often driven by words spoken or attitudes conveyed by parents or other authority figures. Such messages can propel people into careers they hate or relationships that seem doomed to fail. When we live on the fumes of a message sent years ago, they can control us like a drug. We end up playing a role that betrays our originality and satisfies other people's whims, which can be like unstable weather on a summer day. What to do?

I hit it off immediately with Marcus Borg. I've always resonated with his writings and appreciated his person even more. Marcus says that he has spent his life searching for Jesus. He grew up in a traditional Christian environment, which he rejected as a young man. His thirst for knowledge seemed incongruent with the faith of his childhood. Nonetheless, Marcus sought a career in religious scholarship. After years of pursuing Jesus as a historical figure, Marcus was pursued by God. Through a series of transformative experiences, Marcus embraced God in a new and profound way. "These contemplative experiences took place in my late thirties and revealed to me an experiential side of God I had not known," Marcus recalled. These experiences initiated a hunger to reframe and reform his faith into something vibrant that would deny neither his head nor his heart.

I felt our time together was less an interview for this book than a gift for my life. I had a strange sensation that I was looking at myself in the future. It seemed Marcus had traveled a path very similar to the one I was now on. I wanted to slow time down and stay in the moments with Marcus as long as possible. I listened from my heart in hopes that this interview would speak to my own questions and my own struggle to walk the path before me.

A couple of weeks after the interview, an e-mail from Marcus helped me realize that he'd had a similar feeling. He wrote, "I had the sensation I was looking at myself in the past." Here was a picture of a master and an apprentice. I mean this in the way people used to apprentice under masters as they learned an art or a trade. I saw Marcus as one who could mentor me in the art of life. How I longed for the interview to last longer than a few hours.

∿ Dysfunction in ∿ Performance-Driven Living

As I approached forty, I was aware of some rather dysfunctional energy at work in my heart. It seemed these energies had increased in strength over the last couple of years. I found myself more often pulled toward the dysfunction of performance-driven living. I also found myself disappointed when my performance didn't yield the outcome I had expected. Marcus, it became clear, had weathered these same storms. He said, "I was around forty when I discovered I was pretty performance-driven. I felt a tremendous pressure to 'get it all right' in my marriage, parenting, and career." And Marcus continued, "I found myself disappointed that my achievement was less than I desired. I had a lot of ambition as a young man. I wasn't living from the inside out. I was living from the outside in."

When Marcus spoke, I tried to hide the fact that his words had just split me wide open. I flashed a nervous smile that suggested the air was getting thick. Marcus's next few sentences disappeared into a vortex of irrelevancy. I was stuck with the realization that I was living from the lie that my life was not good enough. My incessant attempts to perform my way to something better did not change anything except the level of my frustration. The difference between performance and expression started to become clear as I listened to Marcus.

I recognized that performance was action driven by a need to increase the size of the shallow ego and sustain its never-ending obsession for recognition. Expression, however, was the action that comes from my second authenticity—that reveals my originality and satisfies my desire to create. Performance drives me to pursue action for the sole purpose of enlarging my image, whether it's through a job or a relationship. Even though I know it is wrong for me, I still pursue it because it feeds the bottomless pit of my ego.

Ego-driven performance can also taint authentic action. I end up doing authentic action for the wrong reasons, which then lessens the potency of that action and turns it into another ploy for self-aggrandizement. I might say yes to a speaking engagement, not because I want to serve the audience but because I want to inflate my ego. The more impure my motive, the less my action will serve anyone but myself. Ouch. This was beginning to hurt.

Performance-driven living puts my ego where the Mystery belongs. Instead of participating with the Mystery, I block God's presence and usurp that presence for myself. Marcus put it this way: "The difference between performance and expression is the difference between living one's life radically centered in God versus living centered in the messages of this world. There's enormous freedom in that."

This idea is a favorite theme of Marcus. In his book *Jesus: A New Vision,* he writes:

> To speak of radically centering in God is central to the tradition in which Jesus stood. . . . To say that "centering in God" was the essence of the tradition was thus commonplace; but deliberately to contrast "centering in God" to the centers legitimated by conventional wisdom, indeed conventional wisdom itself, was radical. Yet this is precisely what Jesus did. The central concerns of the conventional wisdom of his day—family, wealth, honor, and religion—were all seen as rival centers. His criticism of them was a call to center in Spirit, and not in culture.[1]

Performance-driven living comes when we focus our lives on one of the rival centers that Marcus named (family, wealth, honor, and religion). These environments are not inherently evil, but none were designed to be the center of life. If I choose to make one of these the center, I suffer the consequences and lose a part of my originality. If this concept seems fuzzy to you, then my suggestion is you simply put it to the test.

Go ahead and center your life on a person and imagine him or her as the entire reason you exist. Try something similar with your job or your religion. Soon enough, you'll discover that life with any of these at the center will cause you strife. At an intuitive level, we know that fully centering on people or things (including self) is dangerous. When a relationship or the next project or the next you-name-it is all-consuming, it leads to a very dark place. This is a place we would all like to avoid as much as possible.

If I'm not careful, my life can narrow down to my latest Amazon book rating. It starts out harmlessly enough. I just want to see how one of my books is doing. The Amazon ranking is one nonscientific way I evaluate how my books are moving. I notice that the ranking is poor, and the spiral begins. I begin checking to see what, if anything, is being said about my books. I blame the marketing department of my publishers (this is a favorite tactic of authors). I assume that my career as a writer is fading and then start to get bored.

See where this can take me? All because I let life narrow itself down to a ranking on a Web page. This can happen quickly and consume me for some time. What consumes you? Can you describe the process that leads you into this dark place of overambition? While we're being honest, let me tell you another of my struggles that will further illustrate the woes that await us when our focus is tainted by a rival center.

Becoming Overambitious

My name is Dave, and I'm an e-mail-aholic. To be more specific about my addiction, I'll name it the Check-the-Messages Syndrome. On a good day, I check messages once an hour. On a bad day, far more often. On a really good day, I do the more appropriate two-times-a-day check. Now granted (here comes my justification for my dysfunction), my work sometimes requires me to be in real-time e-mail contact with people. But the legitimacy of my e-mail need pales in comparison to the number of times I check it. What is going on here?

I don't check my e-mail because I get a cheap thrill out of the process. I check it because of another dysfunction at work in me. Embarrassing though it may be to admit, I check my e-mail often to see if any mail has arrived that would increase my importance or make me feel significant. This could come in a number of forms. For instance, I might receive an e-mail from an important person. This is nice because I can mention to my friends, in a nonchalant way, that I received such an e-mail. "Oh, Dave knows so and so. How impressive that he got an e-mail from her," my friends might think. More than likely, when I name-drop my friends can smell my pride from across the room. But one can always choose to live in denial about how one appears to his friends.

Another good e-mail is one announcing that a desire of mine is about to materialize. This could be a consulting or speaking gig or something else that has the potential to increase my fame. We're now close to the deeper dysfunction. I check my e-mail so often because I grasp at life in order to improve my status, identity, or ego. This woe lies at the heart of performance-driven living. Performance-driven living keeps me bound up in activity for the sole purpose of appearances, namely, the appearance of me in an over-inflated manner. But there's even more.

I also check e-mail too often because performance living is about what I *don't* possess rather than what I *do* possess. The message behind the Check-the-Messages Syndrome is that my life is unimportant and meaningless without the next stimulation. My identity gets wrapped up in the next activity that will remind me of my value. This identity-driven activity is maddening because the next thing will *not* alter me for good. It will simply become the next disappointment—the next result that didn't meet my expectations. The fact is that no e-mail is going to change my life for good or reshape my identity. What reshapes my identity is faithfulness to the pursuit of my second authenticity and the expression that comes as a result.

The energy that drives me to distraction robs me of the joy of appreciating what I have been given. Performance-driven living takes me to a selfish and ungrateful place. I recently put it to a friend this way: "I am sometimes so obsessed about what could be that I lose the joy of what is."

I don't know what action of yours is equivalent to my e-mail dysfunction, but we all have one. You might chuckle at my dysfunction because you do not struggle with e-mail at all. The real question for you is not how you handle your e-mail but what activity in your life leads you to grasp at ego inflation. We grasp at different things. What binds us together is that we all look to prop up the ego through enhancements. This taints our gifts and turns them into a means for selfish ends.

∿ Grasping, Seeking, ∿ and Getting Big Heads

On the surface, grasping and seeking can appear similar, yet the two are worlds apart. *To seek* means we will enter life with a desire to connect to God, others, and life with passion and humility. To grasp is to obsess about or manipulate life and people so that it strengthens the selfish ego.

As Marcus told me, "In my thirties, ambition seemed to serve me well. But then I hit a crisis that changed everything. I was faced with a choice to move out of or stay driven by this performance mode. I took a look at my career and had to admit that it would not be as outstanding as I had hoped. So much of my thirties was about letting go of ambition. At forty, I let go and accepted my life . . . and wouldn't you know a couple years later my career took off."

He laughed and said, "If you want it, you can't have it; if you don't want it, you just might get it."

He laughed again. I forced a smile again, as I did earlier when Marcus had described my life. I was disappointed with how my life was turning out. It was driving me to obsess about book sales and speaking engagements and fame and on and on. Then Marcus relayed a quote from Jung that brought it all home: "The first half of life is about ego development and the second, ego reconnection." I was about to cry.

I blurted, "Okay, Marcus, this is really hitting me hard. I need to talk about this from my own experience. I'm right at this point in my own life." He smiled as if he had been waiting for me to admit this.

"How old are you, Dave?"

"I'm thirty-eight" (which would have been true for another month).

"Well," he laughed. "You have two years to go."

"Yes, I'd better hurry up and get to reconnection." I winced. I felt like a six-year-old who can't print very well watching his teacher write with ease.

I then asked Marcus this question: "What helped you make this journey away from overambition to a life of genuine expression?" I did not expect his next words.

"I learned to be OK with obscurity," said Marcus.

He went on to reemphasize that in his early forties he came to a choice point about his life. He saw his life was not what he had hoped for. He could either come to peace with this or fight against it. (I bristled inwardly at these words, which revealed how much I needed to hear them.) Marcus then told me about his big head—well, sort of.

In the middle of his struggle, Marcus said he had a dream about a man with a big head. The man's head was so disproportionate to his body that it stood way out. One of the messages Marcus took from the dream was that he had an overinflated desire to stand out and be noticed. "I had to come to peace with my own obscurity and that I was of value, even if I wasn't known the way I desired to be."

It all came together for me at this moment. Performance-driven behavior and activity originates from my distaste for obscurity. I want to be seen. I often choose behaviors that will increase my visibility. Conversely, when I live out of authentic expression I am more visible, not because I'm trying to be noticed but because my life is attractive to those around me. The difference is that being noticed is not the primary motivation for expressive and creative action. In expression, I am free to let the outcome be what it will be and produce what it will produce. When I express rather than perform, outcomes do not have to fit my expectations to be meaningful, nor am I driven by the need to be stroked for my contribution.

∿ Peace in Expression ∿

The force behind the desire to create that is part of second authenticity is powerful, but that power can be easily distorted or abused. This is all the more reason why Marcus's words about obscurity hit me. The difference between performance and expression is usually quite clear to me. When I'm in expression mode, I'm at peace. When I'm in performance mode, I'm anything but peaceful. Peace is a barometer of sorts that can reveal how far toward expression or performance I am tilting in the moment.

The beauty of peace is that it is both prescriptive and descriptive. Peace describes a person who is living out of authentic expression, and peace is the virtue that authenticates her action as she does it. The more I experience peace through authenticity, the more peace will infect and influence my action. What a beautiful rhythm. When I internally come to a place of peace about my life and my identity, I am much less concerned about my Amazon ranking or the e-mails of the day. Instead, I am able to invest my energy in my writing, speaking, and coaching. Peace breaks the power of performance-driven living and enables me to relax about things that are out of my control and invest in places where my influence lies.

At times, this internal shift from panic to peace is physiological, emotional, and spiritual. I can actually feel the release of the tension in my body and in my soul. There is a peace point, a letting go, a giving up that allows me to participate more fully in my life. The virtue of peace gives us the possibility of being both involved and detached in our action. We are involved deeply in the expression of our life while detached from the overambition of an ego gone astray.

Cultivating Peace by Ceasing to Strive

In the ancient sacred text of the Old Testament, there is a phrase in Psalm 46 that reads, "Cease striving and know that I am God."[2] This small phrase contains wisdom that helps us make the movement toward peace and authentic expression. When we strive our way through life, our actions lean in the direction of unhealthy performance. Striving wreaks havoc on our ability to experience and express peace. When we strive, we grow uptight, anxious, and unable to sense our deeper originality. We are like a person who thrashes about in a pool, unable to allow anyone the opportunity to save him.

The wisdom of the phrase, "Cease striving and know that I am God," is twofold. First, we are encouraged to choose peace over strife. Second, we are invited to know God who is the Mystery that infuses all things. There is no doubt that the sage who wrote these words meant to link the two ideas together. Simply to live in the presence of the Mystery enables us to abolish strife from our actions. In return, the more at peace we are, the more we are able to sense the presence of the Mystery and the sacred dimension. The opposite is true as well. The less we experience God, the less we experience the peace that emanates from the Mystery. The more we strive, the more difficult it is to sense God's presence.

Marcus told me this: "I see how my life has been lived in the world of oughts and shoulds. I think I acquired from my church upbringing a very strong sense of sin. And that sin was basically failing to live up to the commands of God. This caused me to struggle as a teen with my self and identity. I grew up Lutheran, which at the theological level is a tradition of grace. Luther's experience was breakthrough in nature . . . deliverance from a punitive God. Yet what I received in the church only strengthened the superego, which, for me, became the voice of God."

To cease from striving begins as we learn to disentangle the voice of God from the voice of everyone and everything else. Our lack of peace comes as we internalize a multitude of voices and allow those voices to dominate, distort, distract, and control us. Peace comes when the voices in our lives are at an appropriate volume. If voices increase beyond what is appropriate, we begin to strive in order to satisfy that voice. These voices are often parental, religious, and cultural. Marcus reminded me: "The superego can take a religious form but also can take a secular form. That is, we can be driven by the performance rules of our culture. I see eight-year-olds that are preoccupied with the right name brand. Life under the law means we live under the pressure of the internalized demands."

Take my e-mail dysfunction for example. When the voice of ambition or importance is too loud, my dysfunctional behavior increases. When the voice of ambition increases, it is never satisfied. The more I try to satisfy it, the more my action turns to striving and dysfunctional performance. I spend too much time acting in ways that lead nowhere but to frustration and disappointment. My rigid ego needs the wisdom of Psalm 46: "Cease striving and know that I am God."

The good news in all of this is that peace, ironically, is often the result of strife. Only after our strife has so exhausted us do we open to a more relaxed and authentic posture. It's often as we give up that we find that peace floods in. This takes us back once again to the idea of compost. Even the frustration of our striving is thrown in the compost and can yield the fruit of authentic expression. This is the wonder of how the Mystery works. God can make all things, even striving, into the raw materials for new life and growth.

What is our role in this movement from striving to peace? In a word, surrender. Action is transformed into expression through surrender. It leads us back to a posture of peace and potency. We've all experienced this dynamic at one time or another. We've all said things like, "I finally gave up on trying to change him, and then he changed" or "I quit trying to pursue my dream job, and then the phone rang." It's almost as if striving is an energy that blocks life and our ability to find life and express it more fully. The more we strive, the more the ego whines for more activity that puts it front and center. The maddening cycle overwhelms us, and it is through surrender that we break the cycle and move back to peace and expression.

This idea relates to my Muslim friend's exhortation to die before we die. The death we must experience is the death of the never-satisfied ego that whines its way to more exposure. We are encouraged to turn down the volume on the voices that would support and enhance the shallow ego. "To die before I die" means

I will lessen the grip of the unhealthy ego. In *Jesus: A New Vision,* Borg writes:

> These—the self and the world—are the two great rival cen-
> ters to centering in God, and the path of transformation
> thus involves a dying to both of them. The "world" to
> which one must die is the world of conventional wisdom,
> the world of "culture" with its preoccupying securities; and
> the self which must die is the self-preoccupied self. Then is
> born a self which is centered in God, in Spirit, and not in
> culture.[3]

Marcus's point here is not that culture is wrong or evil. Neither is the self something to eradicate. Notice that he uses the word *pre-occupied* to modify *world* and *self.* This preoccupation is similar to my notion of loudness, of volume. When we are preoccupied with lesser voices, we lose our peace, and action becomes performance-driven. The ancient Jewish sage of Psalm 46 might say, "Don't be pre-occupied with lesser things; center your life in the Divine." This is what transforms our action into expression.

Meditating

We need a way to turn the volume down on our preoccupa-tions with lesser voices. We need a way to cease striving and con-nect with the Mystery. This brings us back to spiritual practice. There is no better way to turn down the volume on the voices of performance than through relaxed and regular spiritual practice. Meditation seems to be tailor-made to help us turn down the voices and live in greater connection to the Mystery.

I hesitate to put meditation in this context, because the great teachers of meditation caution against making meditation a utili-tarian practice—a means to a specific end. Even though the bene-fits of meditation are legion, it is better to see the practice as an end unto itself. The benefits are simply icing on the cake. It might be better to talk about what meditation will produce in us as we practice it. The fruit of meditation is peace and a more authentic expression of the original self.

I have found that the practice of meditation influences more of my life the longer I meditate. When I first began to meditate, I saw it as a practice that was confined to a certain time in my day. I would meditate in the morning and perhaps at night. Meditation was localized to the moments when I was still, yet flexibly focused on the Mystery.

As the years have passed, I have seen meditation influence my life far beyond the time given to sitting still and being quiet. Mediation has become the way in which I keep the volume appropriate on the voices that can preoccupy me during the day. When my practice is consistent, I find it much easier to ignore those voices or put them in the proper perspective. My attitude is more grace-filled and my action more genuine. Meditation done in the morning can change the way I respond to my children or my wife later that afternoon. The longer I meditate, the more I find its fruit at work in my daily situations and circumstances.

∾ How Meditation Made a Difference ∾

Several years back, I used the Prayer of St. Francis during my times of meditation. Some days, I would quietly pray each line and then begin the prayer again. Other days, I would choose one phrase from the prayer and turn it over (gently and flexibly) in my mind and heart. For instance, I would say, "Lord make me an instrument of your peace." Over and over I would turn the phrase. If I became distracted, as all masters of meditation encourage, I would gently come back to the chosen phrase: "Lord make me an instrument of your peace."

I meditated my way through the prayer for months. Soon I found its words starting to shape the texture of my day. I was no longer saying the words; the words were shaping the way I lived. The words of the prayer gave me the opportunity to express my originality in any given moment.

One day, I came home from work to find my boys, who were probably six and eight at the time, fighting in an upstairs bedroom. I was in no mood for this boyish tussle. The day had been long and difficult, and I felt a little like a hissing cat. As I shut the front door, the volume in the bedroom above me increased. Like all brothers, my boys know just how to irritate and inflame the other. The fighting increased, and so did the temperature of my blood. I decided I would stomp up the stairs. Surely, the sound of my intimidating five-foot-eight-inch, 165-pound physique stomping up the stairs would do the trick. Yeah, right. As I rounded the corner, my boys were close to blows, and I was close to blowing my stack. I had every intention of yelling, and I do mean yelling: *"All right, that's it. You get in your room, and you get in yours. I want this stopped right now. Do you hear me?"* I rehearsed the words as I rounded the top stairs and approached my boys.

Just as I was winding up to practice a little domination and take control of the situation, I inwardly heard this phrase: "Lord make me an instrument of your peace." I froze. Not now God, I thought to myself. Not now, God. I don't want to be an instrument of your peace now. This is the wrong moment. The meditation I had practiced for months brought me to a choice point. Would I offer my boys a manipulative and domineering kind of discipline? Would I become an instrument of peace as I disciplined them? The choice was mine. The practice of meditation, specifically the Prayer of St. Francis, was influencing moments of my life far beyond the act of meditation. It was giving me an opportunity to express a more genuine heart in a moment that desperately needed just that. What to do?

I'm happy to say that I chose wisely that time. The prayer enabled me to surrender, find peace, and give my boys a better picture of a father. Instead of control, I gave them a tender correction that helped each to see the situation with different eyes. More important, I became part of the solution by getting down on the floor and playing a game with both of them. We talked and laughed, and I sensed I had given my boys a more authentic expression of love, discipline, and gentleness. This came directly as a result of meditation and its influence on my heart.

Meditation turned down the other voices of control and manipulation and increased my connection to the Mystery when I needed it most. I'm not happy to confess that there have been many other moments when I've chosen not to respond to the invitation that comes through meditation. Plenty of times I've said, "Forget it. I don't want to be your instrument of peace." This is the dance of life. We learn to be both receptive and surrendered to the Mystery. Sometimes it goes well. Sometimes it doesn't. Meditation increases my desire to live more from that receptive posture. I've included the Prayer of St. Francis so you can try using it in your meditation as well.

> *Lord, make me an instrument of thy peace.*
> *Where there is hatred, let me sow love;*
> *Where there is injury, pardon;*
> *Where there is doubt, faith;*
> *Where there is despair, hope;*
> *Where there is darkness, light;*
> *Where there is sadness, joy.*
> *O divine Master, grant that I may not*
> *so much seek*
> *To be consoled as to console,*
> *To be understood as to understand,*

To be loved, as to love;
For it is in giving that we receive;
It is in pardoning that we are pardoned;
It is in dying to self that we are born
To eternal life.

What I call meditation, Marcus calls contemplation. In his book *The Heart of Christianity,* he writes:

> The purpose of contemplation is to sit silently in the presence of God, of "what is." Contemplation typically involves the repetition of a mantra, whether a single word, a short phrase, or a series of short phrases. But the words are not to be meditated on; rather, they are used to give the mind a focus so that the rest of the self can sink into silence. . . . Ultimately, the purpose of contemplative prayer is to descend to the deepest level of the self, of the heart, where we open out into the sea of being that is God.[4]

In light of that description, read this ancient wisdom once again: "Cease striving and know that I am God."

Contemplative meditation invites me to set aside a specific amount of time and sit still in the sea of being that is God. The more this type of meditation is practiced, the more that sea of being is available beyond the time of meditation—like when your children are fighting. The sea of being opens to us as we work and create. It becomes a sea of peace we can live out of that creates in us sensitivity to God and to others.

For Marcus, much of this meditative experience and expression of life comes as he teaches around the country and in the academic world. Marcus said, "I experience an awful lot of intimacy with my audience. I imagine it's a little like what a solo musician feels when they begin and the audience and musician become one with the music."

Several years ago, I attended a seminar Marcus taught. I can confirm his analogy of being a musician. Marcus began the seminar with a time of communal meditation. The spirit of the meditation expanded beyond the moments of practice and became the environment for the entire day. The dynamic is available to each of us as we express ourselves day in and day out. Meditative expression comes from the heart and changes the world around us. It is the action we long to experience and manifest. It is the seeker's way.

NOTES

1. Borg, M. *Jesus: A New Vision: Spirit, Culture and the Life of Discipleship*. New York: HarperCollins, 1987, p. 111.

2. *New American Standard Bible*. Chicago: Moody Press, 1977 (Psalm 46:10).

3. Borg, 1987, p. 113.

4. Borg, M. *The Heart of Christianity*. San Francisco: HarperSanFrancisco, 2003, pp. 198–199.

CHAPTER VII

From Segregation to Community

Seeker: Joan Chittister is a Benedictine nun who has been a leading voice on spirituality for over twenty-five years. She is executive director of Benetvision, a resource and research center for contemporary spirituality located in Erie, Pennsylvania. Chittister is a noted national and international lecturer whose keynote addresses and conferences focus on women in church and society, human rights, peace and justice, and contemporary religious life and spirituality.

Have you thought about Joan Chittister?"

Toward the end of my time with Marcus Borg, I told him I still had to find a person to interview for the chapter on longing to move from segregation to community. I mentioned to him that I wanted a female perspective on the longing, and he suggested Joan Chittister. I was familiar with Joan's writings and had even made initial contact with her about the possibility of an interview. For some reason, I hadn't firmed up that possibility.

Four days later, as I sat with Phil Gulley and Jim Mulholland, we discussed the concept for this book. I again shared that I was searching for a final female voice to include in the book. Out of the blue, Phil said, "Ya know, I've just read some articles by Joan Chittister. She's great. Have you considered her?"

Now, I can be slow when it comes to reading the fingerprints of the Mystery. But even I got this one. I was *supposed* to talk to Joan Chittister. A few hours later, while I sat in the Indianapolis airport, I phoned Sister Joan's office and set up the interview.

Two months passed. It was finally time to meet Joan.

I was sitting in a Starbucks in Pittsburgh, watching the snow fall harder and harder. The roads from Pittsburgh to Erie (where Joan lives) were treacherous, and people were being advised not to travel. The interview would not happen on this snowy day. As I watched the snow accumulate, I realized just how intriguing the endeavor of getting to Joan was becoming. Two separate people in different settings, in different cities, had suggested Joan as the sixth interview. Then, on the day of the interview, the weather foiled my plans. I wondered what Joan had to share with me that was so important. I would soon find out.

I called Joan as the snow fell, and we lamented the conditions of the road. We then looked at our calendars and determined that there was literally one day possible for the interview. If it didn't work on that day, it wasn't going to work at all. By this point, I was determined to get to Erie and interview Joan, no matter what. I did.

I sat in Joan's warm, simply furnished office on that cold December day, waiting for her to appear. I could see a room in the back that appeared to be where Joan studied and maybe wrote. My heart beat a little faster. I waited.

"I'm not sure what's keeping Joan. She should be here by now," her assistant told me in apologetic tones. Joan was nowhere to be found. I waited.

No Joan.

Her assistant checked on me every so often as I sat there. She assured me that this was very unusual. "You have no idea," I whispered to myself as I thought about the journey to reach Joan. In fact, a deep peace came over me as I inwardly recounted the steps to Joan's office. It didn't matter when Joan arrived. I would take any time given, even if it was just five minutes.

I waited.

I had a few of Joan's books with me. As I flipped through them, it became clear to me why Joan was exactly the right person to talk with about the longing for relational integration and community. Years earlier, I had read her work and knew of her desire for authentic relationships of equality and grace. Consider these words from *Wisdom Distilled from the Daily:*

> In the Far East there is a traditional image of the difference between heaven and hell. In hell, the ancients said, people have chopsticks one yard long so they cannot possibly reach their mouths. In heaven, the chopsticks are also one yard long—but, in heaven the people feed one another.[1]

Chittister goes on to say:

> It is not a case, in other words, of what we have in life. It is
> a case of what we do with it that determines the quality of
> the communal life we lead. Benedictine spirituality is intent
> on the distribution of self for the sake of the other. But it is
> intent as well on the presence of the other for my sake as
> well.[2]

Joan's simple message: we were not designed to seek alone.

Authentic spirituality is experienced in community. The real
gifts of the spiritual life yield to us as we seek together. The journey is best traveled in the company of others who round out, even
challenge, our personal spirituality. All sorts of trouble awaits us if
our spiritual life is overly privatized. We lose the wonder of other
perspectives and the scrutiny that fellow travelers bring to our own
views on matters of faith and life. Without others' ideas, we are
confined to our own, and this can lead to either selfishness or self-
righteousness. With spiritual friends, we are able to appreciate a
spirituality that is enhanced by the texture of their views and experiences.

Don't misunderstand me here. I'm not suggesting that your
spiritual life should be nothing more than the collection of other
people's ideas. Communities of faith need to be populated by
unique individuals who stand on their own two feet. When this is
not the case, the community too easily degenerates into a narrow-
minded club that works hard to keep the right people in and the
wrong people out. This is groupthink at its worst. It is a groupthink that wraps its tentacles around good people and turns them
toward bigotry, prejudice, and exclusivity. What is needed is a spirituality grounded in both the communal and the personal. It is the
rhythm of both that provides us the best environment in which to
journey as seekers of the Mystery.

Joan finally appeared. There had been a mix-up in communication, and she was not aware of my arrival. She whisked into the room with an apology and an infectious energy that immediately set the tone for our dialogue. It didn't take long for me to sense Joan's passion for genuine community.

As we got to know each other, I remembered again the rather serendipitous way I had found Joan. I smiled while she articulately and fervently explained her passion for the seeker's life. She was putting finishing touches on her latest book, *Called to Question*. In that book, readers would be allowed to peek into Joan's journals and her own quest for a deepening and communal spirituality that is built not on certainty but on life as quest and question. It also would reveal her passion to remove the obstacles that keep us from each other, that keep us separated rather than integrated.

∿ The Insidious Nature of Segregation ∿

When I asked Joan to tell me a little about her story, one of her first anecdotes was about a day when she came home from school and heard her mother's familiar question, "Joan, what did you learn at school today?" Most days when asked that question, Joan would overflow with curiosity and delight as she shared her latest discoveries with her mother. On this particular day, Joan had a very serious and troubling piece of information to share. What she had learned at school shook the very foundation of her life and would become a defining day in her life and vocation.

"Today I learned that Protestants don't go to heaven," Joan said to her mother.

Joan told me that she was a deeply spiritual child who loved her Catholic school and the milieu it provided for learning and spiritual life. On this day, she was torn between her love for the nuns who taught her and deeper love she could not betray. She asked her mother, "Do you think my teacher is right? Are Protestants kept out of heaven?" The question was important to Joan far beyond theological considerations. Theology played no part in her concern. You see, her father was a Protestant.

So many things divide and segregate us. Our beliefs and creeds, ethnicity and political persuasions, backgrounds and personalities—all can become walls that keep us from each other. We erect these walls to increase our own feelings of assurance and security. If we can assure ourselves that our group is "the group" or our way is "the way," then we can create a comfortable grid by which to judge and contain the rest of the world. You either fit or you don't. You're either in or out. You're either one of us or you're not. The world from this view is a dangerous place, and we gain safety only as we insulate ourselves from those who are different. In *Called to Question,* Joan writes:

> There are some things, we learn early, that are never to be challenged. They are absolute. They come out of the fountain of eternal truth. And they are true because some else said they are true. So we live in someone else's answers for a long time.[3]

Such rigidly defined views of the world feel safe because we can rest in the assurance that we're right and connected directly to God. Who is going to argue with God? Ultimately, such a view breeds segregation because the same God that makes us right makes others wrong.

"What do you think, Joan? Was this Sister right?" Joan's mother waited for her reply.

"I don't believe it's true; the Sister was wrong," Joan replied.

"Then why do you think your teacher said this?" her mother questioned.

"Because," Joan responded, "she doesn't know Daddy."

"Well then, Joan, tell her that," came the reply.

With those words, Joan popped back into the present moment of our interview, leaned forward, and said to me, "And I've been telling people that ever since."

Joan's passion for community is grounded in the reality that it is our misunderstanding of each other that breeds segregation and division. Her life has been and is a voice for those who are segregated by and from the powerful. She has a particular desire to help us understand the equality men and women share, the gifts each brings, and the distortions that can ruin those gifts and equality. She is fervent about her call to champion equality and the dangers that have arisen because of segregation between men and women. She wrote in *Called to Question:*

> The spiritual fallout of the loss of the woman's agenda in the public arena is incalculable. Governments attend to male agendas and make decisions according to male perspectives and male value systems. The church inherited a male God and all the implications that go with it for marriage law, social hierarchies, sacramental systems and ecclesiastical pomp and power. . . . As a result, the major social systems of the world have been working with only half the resources of the human race. Theology and ministry have lost the wisdom of the feminine. So much for Mary of Nazareth and the God who is "pure spirit," neither male nor female but the essence of both.[4]

It is undeniable that the spirit of segregation has influenced the relationships of men and women, not to mention blacks and whites and the ubiquitous religious segregation that is at the center of so many wars. Segregation is abolished, not through the elimination of our differences but rather through a new relationship and conversation in the midst of those differences. Grace-filled dialogue enables us to learn from each other and challenge each other to live more holistic and peace-centered lives. These relationships require an intentional cultivation that honors our diversities yet seeks constantly to build common ground. This is what creates true community. And seekers know the importance of community.

As we grow in our spirituality, we increasingly desire to be unique as an individual while simultaneously eradicating the prejudices that lead to exclusive thinking and living. We can embrace a view of the world that allows for personal identity and conviction without the intolerance that labels and negates those who are different. We all want to be accepted for both the person we are and the one we are becoming. We too often do not give that gift in return. The seeker's path is one of reciprocity. We give the gift of acceptance as much as we desire to receive it. We long to experience the treasure hidden in those who are not like us. Rather than seeing difference as a threat, seekers celebrate it as the Technicolor of the Mystery.

Technicolor and diverse community are neither an anemic blending of differences nor a pseudo-agreement that leads to an existence free of convictions. They are instead characterized by an encounter of two people that leads each one to transformation. Each is sharpened by the variations encountered in the other. In authentic community, we do not become like each other or force smiles of agreement; rather, our encounter enables us to become ourselves—our second-authenticity selves.

Community, as I've described it, comes as we allow the differences in others to press on our hearts and thus shape our hearts in profound ways. It also comes as we resist the differences of others and appreciate those differences without owning them for ourselves. This is the true meaning of encounter. When we encounter someone, we allow the other "in" and we also "counter" in order to remain true to our own path. Community is the art of knowing when to allow another in and when to counter.

The community we speak of in this chapter may or may not lead to agreement at the level of religious belief. Religious agreement is not the aim of such community. The aim is alignment of the heart, of the values and longings that make us human. The paradox is that we must hold fast to the convictions of our hearts without holding those convictions in a manner that leads to division, exclusion, or segregation. When convictions are held with passion, but not in a divisive manner, those convictions can bring alignment with others, even if they disagree with our conclusions. When beliefs are used to draw lines for the purpose of security or significance, it leads to the dangers of segregation. Everyone loses.

I have at times been saddened by Christians who describe anyone who doesn't believe the way they do as "lost." This kind of thinking has led some Christians to establish relationships for the sole purpose of converting people. The agenda is set before any words are spoken. There is little, if any, thought that the person from the other culture could enhance the Christian's spirituality in any way. The "other" is simply in a lost condition and is in need of conversion.

Funny, I don't see Jesus operating this way in his life. He had no agenda to convert people to anything but the love and grace of God and the abundant life they'd always wanted.

Jesus sought out people with an open heart, not those in the "right" group or with the "correct" belief system. Some of Jesus' highest praise came for people outside his own faith tradition—a gentile woman who pleaded with Jesus to heal her daughter and a Roman centurion who had faith like no one else Jesus had encountered. Jesus didn't tell these two people they were "lost" because they were outside his tradition. No. Jesus instead celebrated the faith they already were demonstrating. This didn't go over well for some in his tradition. In fact, it infuriated them. Jesus tore down the walls of religious segregation that had been so carefully constructed. Should we not do the same?

It was this same kind of segregation that Joan discovered as a young child. In her teacher's view, beliefs became the basis for judgments pronounced on entire groups. This is one reason beliefs cannot be the centerpiece of faith but only a part of the journey toward faith. When ideas or doctrines become top priority, there is little choice but to segregate from those who don't agree. When beliefs are fuel for the search, they can be both personal convictions and arenas of exploration with those who hold different views. This is the challenge for spiritual seekers who find themselves living in the twenty-first century.

The experience and discipline of diverse and grace-filled community is so critical to the seeker's path. Without it, we cannot learn true human acceptance of the other. We do not develop the capacity to give or receive gifts from other people who are different from us. This kind of community is critical to our future. This all sounds very good, but what is required to create such nourishing communities?

∿ The Value of Making ∿ Space for the Other

To integrate instead of segregate, we have to make space for each other. This relational space is vital for two hearts to find alignment and discover the wisdom each has to offer. Space begins in the heart and moves outward as a display of honor and value. No real space can be made outwardly until it has been made inwardly. If I harbor prejudice against you in my heart, the outer space I grant you will be contrived and manipulative in nature. We first make space in our heart so that the space we give each other is grace-filled and genuine.

In American culture, we've lost sight of this concept. We haven't made enough space in our hearts to honor and value those around us. We don't, for example, hold much space in our hearts for the elderly. In ancient cultures, the elderly were revered as repositories of wisdom and experience. Too often today, they are viewed as inconvenient because they can no longer hold their own. We don't have time or make space for their vulnerable, valuable wisdom.

Examples of a lack of heart-space abound in our culture, particularly in gender and race relations. Though American society has come a long way in race and gender issues, there is still a subtle and sometimes not-so-subtle attitude that rears its head and influences action. For example, an African American woman might be passed over for a promotion or be treated differently in a neighborhood simply because of her skin color. To suggest that this kind of thing doesn't happen anymore is to live in illusion.

Even when we make space for each other, our attitudes toward each other in that space can ruin it. The surge of talk radio and politics-based television shows that often become shouting matches turns a space that could foster debates of ideas into a space that denigrates people. The creation of space is therefore not enough. When we create space with goodwill, it enables us to suspend judgment toward each other and find the unique wisdom each of us holds. This begins with respect and reverence for the other—attitudes that are so often lost in our disposable and distracted society.

In *Wisdom Distilled from the Daily,* Joan writes about the Benedictine heart and the space that heart is exhorted to make for all people.

Everyone—everyone—is received as Christ. Everyone receives a warm answer—on the phone, at the door, in the office. Sarcasm has no room here. Put downs have no room here. One-upmanship has no room here. Classism has no room here. The Benedictine heart is to be a place without boundaries, a place where the truth of the oneness of all things shatters all barriers, a point where all the differences of the world meet and melt, where Jew and Greek, slave and free, woman and man all come together as equals.[5]

Joan then captures the seeker's desire for integration:

But whatever happens to the heart is the beginning of revolution. When I let strange people and strange ideas into my heart, I am beginning to shape a new world. Hospitality of the heart could change American domestic policies. Hospitality of the heart could change American foreign policy. Hospitality of the heart could make my world a world of potential friends rather than a world of probable enemies.[6]

For seekers, a space that begins in the heart moves outward until those around us are changed and blessed by that space, which enables the seeker to open her heart to those around her. The gift flows in both directions. We are enriched by each other and yet remain distinct and unique. This vision of community requires that we consider those things in our hearts that keep us from mutual openness—the pride, fear, and control that desensitize us toward those who are different. We must take the transformation of these vices seriously if we are to honor each other as bearers of a divine life.

Making Space Through Listening

One critical practice needed to open up our hearts toward each other—and shun the dysfunctions that lead to segregation—

is listening. I do not mean simply hearing the words of another with tolerance. Joan reflects on listening this way:

> Listening is a life-giving act. So many people have never been heard their whole lives. They have raged against the deafness with alcohol and temper tantrums and sex and social paralysis but even then no one has noticed the message. We are all trying to be heard. I must listen more and better to everyone.[7]

When we listen from the heart, we offer each other two gifts. First, we assume a posture of receptivity and mutuality; together we become learners on the seeker's path. And then this receptivity and mutuality allow us to encounter each other fully as human beings. Rather than approach each other through sterile beliefs or ideologies, seekers encounter each other with a desire to learn from the other's life experiences and unique view of the world. With this posture, the other person becomes a gift to honor and learn from rather than to manipulate and change in a way that suits our own ideas and tastes.

Listening as a Learner

The word Jesus used to describe his followers was *disciple,* which means "one who is a learner." Many strands of modern Christianity have used the word to mean "one who learns correct doctrine" or "one who learns how to walk the straight and narrow." But it implies much more. To be a learner is first to be ignorant. Without a healthy kind of ignorance—a curiosity to seek more than what we already know—there is nothing to learn and no reason to listen. Blessed are the curious, for they will inherit a more robust faith. Too many religious people, from every tradition, are anything but learners, anything but curious. They believe they have life figured out because of the superiority of their religious system. Certainty causes rigidity, which is the death knell of curiosity and community.

When I approach you as a learner, I draw near to you with an understanding that I do not know everything, and I do not hold all the answers. My curiosity and receptivity create a space for you—a space where you can teach me. I'm interested in you because I truly believe you have wisdom to offer me that will round out my own growth. I can then respond to what I hear, free of manipulation or antagonism. When I respond, I do so, not to convince you of my superiority but to increase the wisdom of your journey as well. It is a give-and-take that moves each of us forward.

The years I've spent as a counselor and consultant have reaffirmed, for me, the importance of listening. And I've discovered that a person's ability to listen is directly connected to his or her humility: a person who believes she has much to learn listens more intently; one who is a know-it-all listens less intently.

Many of our relational troubles are the result of our inability to listen because we believe we are right. I have seen the devastation that occurs when couples, families, and business partners will not admit failure and have lost the quality of receptivity that is characteristic of a learner.

When we believe we have little to learn, we close ourselves off to the wonder and wisdom of the other. If we think others have nothing to teach us, then all we can do is try to create space in which to convince them that we're right. Perhaps this is what caused Sister Joan's teacher to condemn all Protestants to hell. Perhaps she was too closed off to the wonder of other people and too focused on a theological viewpoint she knew so well.

How easy it is to judge another because we think we've got life all figured out. Now we can see that all of the longings in this book not only influence our life but shape how we treat others as well. This may be why Jesus invited people to become childlike—

to approach everything with what the Zen tradition calls the beginner's mind.

Richard Rohr writes,

> One of Jesus' favorite visual aids is a child. Every time the disciples get into head games, he puts a child in front of them. He says the only people who can recognize and be ready for what he's talking about are the ones who come with the mind and heart of a child. It's the same reality as the beginner's mind. . . . We have to pray for the grace of the beginner's mind. We need to say with the blind man, "I want to see."[8]

Beginners are in touch with what they don't know more than what they do know. To seek in community means I seek with a beginner's mind and heart—a heart that makes space for the Mystery to work in diverse relationships.

Listening Through Life

It's essential that we listen to each other through our life experiences. To listen through life experiences means that I honor the context, history, and circumstances of your life as important to our relationship. I don't make rash judgments based on surface appearances but seek to understand how your experiences have shaped you and continue to shape you—to see how those experiences have helped to create your view of the world. I'm not quick to tell you how to live, but I am quick to listen to your story and learn from that story.

Segregation happens as a result of ideas formed in a vacuum. This was the essence of what Joan was saying when she told her mother, "She's wrong, Mommy, because she doesn't know Daddy." Even though Joan could not articulate it at a young age, she was saying, "Your judgment is based on ideas you've conceived without any real experience with this group of people" or "Your judgment is based on ideas you've conceived without any real experience with this group of people, except one or two specimens."

Segregation can be based on judgments made only on the basis of what someone has heard about a particular person or group of people or because of very limited exposure to unfortunate examples of that group. Neither kind of judgment leads to integration, much less to healthy and authentic community.

Seekers live their way to integration with those who are different. Their judgments are made in the context of daily life, not in the vacuum of limited experience and worldview. They don't form opinions or convictions about others through the radio or TV or through the advice of a leader. No. Instead, they enter relationships in order to understand and appreciate those they encounter. Community comes when we get to know the stranger in the context of life and honor that life before seeking to enhance it. How often we make judgments on entire groups of people when we don't have one friend from that group. We've simply formed opinions based on flimsy perceptions or on the advice of a misguided friend or leader. We have no genuine life experience with the very people we choose to label or condemn.

I grew up thinking that Muslims were people to fear and mistrust. I was never around Muslims, nor did I have an opportunity to confirm or deny my ideas. I simply picked them up from others and never questioned them. Recently, my family and I have come to know many Muslims at the school where my wife teaches. Funny, the Muslims I now know look nothing like my pre-existing picture of them, which existed without knowing *one* Muslim. I have found the Muslims I've met to be humble, kind, devout, a bit legalistic, and some of the most giving people I've ever met. What has changed my view? *I've spent time with them in the context of everyday life.*

"Listening through the earpiece of life" means we get to know the stranger in the context of that stranger's life. My family has shared meals with our Muslim friends and important moments (my wife more than I). Through these moments, my perception has changed, and I now see how much my Muslim friends have to teach me. I am making a space for them, and it is enhancing my own path.

One Christmas Eve, we invited a Muslim family over to our house. We talked and laughed, and my boys played pool with the husband. We had dinner and then took them to a neighborhood in our city to see Christmas lights. During our time together, we shared things that were important to us as Christians and Muslims. We exchanged gifts, and my family learned a few Turkish words.

Just prior to dinner, I asked the husband if he would pray for our meal. I could feel the objections of many of my Christian friends, even though none were present. I asked him anyway. "I will pray, but then I must translate the prayer so that you know what I said," he responded. We smiled. He prayed in his native tongue. The only word I recognized was Allah, which I thought was the best word to recognize—the word that bound us together.

After he had finished, we began to pass the food. "I must translate my prayer," he reminded us. We listened. "I thanked God for friends and for the time God has given us. I also asked God that we would have as many thankful thoughts toward God as there are breaths being taken in this moment." A peace settled over the table and over our hearts. This did not fit my perception of Muslims. How can this be? This man is pliable and open to God; his heart is soft and receptive. God's presence was palpable through him. Later, my wife and I commented on how our friend's prayer made our prayers look ridiculous—like selfish Americans who use words like *bless* and *give* way too often.

By living life together with these particular Muslims, I am learning to listen to them through our times together, eating and drinking and laughing and celebrating. As the distance decreases, understanding increases. All of this doesn't make me want to become Muslim or change all my views to fit theirs. But it has shattered my prejudice and created in me a receptivity to find God wherever God is to be found, not just where I decide God can be found. Ultimately, it transforms me into a more authentic seeker and more compassionate person.

∿ The Conversation of Seekers ∿

Beyond honoring all people, seekers are interested in traveling the spiritual path with others, both those who share their beliefs and those who do not. If there is one thing we need in the twenty-first century, it is people from different traditions who make community while maintaining their diversity. For too long, the only conversation many people have had with those of different faiths is about conversion. We really must get beyond this. The ins and outs of the evangelistic efforts of any faith tradition are beyond the purview of this book, but they are worth noting.

I am not about to pronounce judgment on one who feels called to share his faith in order to invite another to consider that faith tradition. This is a natural part of believing that you possess good news. We evangelize each other in all kinds of everyday ways, from movies to hair products. We like to talk about things that have made a difference in our lives, yet if this is our only conversation, we miss the richness we can bring to each other. Seekers enter relationships with others, not to convert them but to travel the road together as friends and seekers of the Mystery.

Even within a tradition, it is sometimes hard to converse with those who not agree on what that tradition is and should be.

I am most attuned to the ridiculous infighting that goes on in Christianity over things like doctrines, appropriate versions of the Bible, and social issues. Christians, who say they are marked by radical love, end up despising each other and verbally attacking each other over these differences. Some make a living at it. How can this be? It's time for a renaissance of conversation with those in and out of our traditions. It's time we move away from segregation (without losing distinction) and toward integration (without losing diversity). This is the passion of the seeker.

Perhaps a good starting point for this renaissance in conversation should be the six longings (and others) that are important to life and spirituality. I would encourage seekers to truly listen to the faith stories of others in order to celebrate them, learn from them, and enhance them through our own stories. I also would encourage seekers to allow others' diversity to take them deeper into their own convictions and beliefs for the purpose of reformation and purification of those beliefs and convictions. This is what my Muslim friends are teaching me. It's a lesson I need to learn and will be learning for years to come. My hope is that seekers will listen to each other's insights and allow those insights to shape their hearts. I also encourage seekers to remain true to the convictions that make them what they are. We need a messier and more dynamic conversation that will require us to remain awake, pliable, compassionate, thoughtful, and appropriately challenging. All of this can be done with a spirit of grace that should mark us as human beings made in the image of God. This is the integration we can find on the seeker's way.

NOTES

1. Chittister, J. *Wisdom Distilled from the Daily: Living the Rule of St. Benedict Today.* New York: HarperCollins, 1990, p. 42.

2. Chittister, 1990, p. 42.

3. Chittister, J. *Called to Question: A Spiritual Memoir.* Chicago: Sheed and Ward, 2004, p. 4.

4. Chittister, 2004, p. 153.

5. Chittister, 1990, pp. 127–128.

6. Chittister, 1990, p. 128.

7. Chittister, 2004, p. 122.

8. Rohr, R. *Everything Belongs: The Gift of Contemplative Prayer.* New York: Crossroad Publishing, 1999, p. 31.

Epilogue:
Starting a Seekers' Group

Almost ten years ago, I started a group that has become like family. At the time, I was pastor at a church in Pittsburgh—a church I love very much. The group began as a place to explore spiritual practices such as prayer, solitude, silence, and journaling. We read a book on spiritual practice and cultivated the practices in the book over a two-to-three-month period.

Because of the success of that group, I started several more. Each group explored spiritual practices. All but two stopped meeting when our exploration of the initial book concluded; these two decided to continue meeting, and one has met for nearly two years. The other is in its tenth year. We call ourselves the Seekers' Group.

This group has become, for me, an icon for what many seekers are hungry to experience. It is a place where we can explore, encourage, complain, vent, and celebrate life through our longings and desires. We do this with the sacred in mind and heart. Although we are all Christians, we are more than willing to seek beyond our faith tradition. This willingness has changed the texture of our faith and how we express it. Each of us has been (and is) on a path that draws us together and yet allows us to maintain our unique perspectives and convictions.

∿ What Drew Us Together ∿

If I had to point to one dynamic that drew my group together and has sustained us through the years, it would be holy discontent. Every person was dissatisfied in some way with faith and spirituality; all were looking for a place to feel safe with this dynamic and explore it with others who felt the same. Some had reached this discontent through a very specific life circumstance; others wrestled with the easy answers of their childhood tradition. This discontent led each one to the search for more. In that search, we found each other.

Amazing. If you find yourself in a place similar to the one I've described here, it is likely that the Mystery has already seen fit to supply you with other people on a similar journey. Who might those others be? The first way to discover this is to pay attention. Listen to the conversations of those around you. Listen for the language of the longings we explored in this book. Listen for holy discontent.

As you listen attentively in the days ahead, you will find yourself drawn to certain people whose language will tell you they are seekers as well. Share your longings with them. Share this book with them. Allow your commonality to grow. Don't worry if you don't agree on everything. That's impossible. The aim here is not to participate in an answers group but a group seeking more than answers. As you get to know each other on the level of the seeker, enlarge the circle. Each one of you knows others who are interested in the same kind of fellowship. Share with those friends what you're discovering, and then take a risk. Have a seekers' party.

You have to get this group of seekers together. Let them know, prior to the party, why you want everyone to meet. If the party is made up of only you and your friend, then throw the party anyway. Two is a party. Go to Starbucks. This will increase the party mood. You will soon find that two turn into three, and multiply from there. But the aim is not to form a huge group. If you have ten or fifteen people come, great. If you decide at the party to become a seekers' group, you may want to create two groups. If a seekers' group gets too big, the potency of the dialogue is diminished.

At your party, share again why you've gathered. Let people tell about their own journey and hear the stories of others. Propose the idea of becoming a group that would meet regularly to explore the seeker's path and the longings that accompany it. People, of course, will want to know what this group will do when it meets. Let me give you some ideas.

◡ What My Seekers' Group Does ◡

The people in my group are readers. Being a reader need not be a prerequisite for participation in the group you form, but readers tend to find topics that seekers are interested in. My group's format is fairly straightforward most of the time. We pick a book that taps into the longings we all share. We then read the book and dialogue around its content. Sometimes it takes us two or three months to get through a book; others we finish in one meeting.

We meet once a month. Your group may decide to meet twice a month or even more frequently. Make sure you can sustain the frequency you decide on for the long haul.

My group reads books as the way into the dialogue about the seeker's path. We have read scores of books over the years. Occasionally, we've also taken field trips. After reading a couple of Thomas Merton's books, we decided to go to a monastery and rub shoulders with monks. We took our seeking on the road.

On a couple of occasions, our group watched movies together and then discussed the seeker's way found in the movies. Your group may want to do this more often. My suggestion is that you watch the movie before you come to the group. If you want to watch the movie together and then discuss its messages, that's fine, too, but that significantly increases the amount of time needed for the meeting.

Maybe your group will simply take a topic or current event as a way into the dialogue. Maybe you will incorporate some activity (the possibilities are endless) as your portal into the conversation. Be creative and experiment early on. You will soon discover your group settling into a kind of medium that works best for all the members. Break that routine every so often so that it does not grow stale. If you're readers, occasionally do something different to keep your communal seeking fresh.

∽ The Kinds of Seekers in a Group ∽

I mentioned earlier that my group is made up of Christians. The people in your group may not share the same faith tradition. Because of where I am in my journey today, if I were starting a new group, I would want it to include Muslims, Buddhists, and members of other religious groups. To me, the essence of being a seeker is being willing to explore beyond the boundaries of one tradition. The purpose of meeting is not to convert each other but to round each other out, no matter the faith tradition. I know some will not agree with me here, and that's fine. You must decide this for yourself.

If your group is made up of people from different faith traditions, you will need to agree that your differences will become a wonderful part of the dynamic of the group rather than a detraction from it. The group is not meant to be a place where people convince others as to the superiority of their own tradition. If a person takes the group down that road, then he or she needs to be gently shown that this is not the purpose. The person can choose whether to stay, given this more inclusive focus.

Books can be read from each tradition, with an eye toward the group's shared longings or the way in which the book brings members in tune with their own faith and spirituality. Many books transcend religious beliefs and could move the group into the dialogue without placing religion at the center of it. A book like *The Five People You Meet in Heaven,* by Mitch Albom, would be an example.[1] Many novels or short-story collections could be used as well. Or you could start with this book.

If your group is made up of people from the same tradition, you face different challenges. First, though you will initially find agreement at the belief level, you could easily succumb to groupthink, which occurs when a group falls into a kind of manipulative alignment. Either out of fear or other powerful forces, no one is willing to challenge the norms of the group. The very nature of a seekers' group is antithetical to groupthink. If the people in the group are not safe and free to share differences of conviction and belief, then the search is over and conformity has set in.

In both types of groups, it is imperative that uniformity of belief *not* become a prerequisite for group health. It is the diversity and curiosity of the group that will enable it to thrive and allow the members to grow. With this in mind, it is essential that the group members understand the dynamics of dialogue as an art form. Dialogue is a very particular kind of conversation in which the aim is the discovery of a common pool of meaning, not the disintegration of ideas through argument or control.

There are many good books on dialogue. I recommend Bill Isaac's *Dialogue and the Art of Thinking Together* as a possibility.[2] Although Isaacs talks a great deal about the application of dialogue to business environments, his general descriptions of dialogue are thoughtful and practical.

∿ A Crash Course in Dialogue ∿

Some of the most important components of dialogue are discovery, suspension, and pliability. The aim of a seekers' group in dialogue is to discover the path of the seeker. The group must come to its conversations with the hearts of adventurers and explorers. Questions to ask might include:

What can we find that will enhance our lives as seekers?
Where is the life in this book and in our current conversation?
What can I learn from you because of the diversity you bring to
    this moment?

These are questions of discovery.

Being able to "suspend" during dialogue is the ability to withhold judgment so that the discovery process can occur. If a group member shuts down the conversation out of fear or insecurity, discovery cannot proceed. There is a kind of grace needed in dialogue that enables the conversation to meander its way to insight. Deep listening and authentic questions are essential to this process. The more statements dominate the landscape of the conversation, the less suspension is likely. Each seeker needs to monitor his or her heart throughout the dialogue to avoid usurping the group, wittingly or unwittingly. Conclusions can, in fact, be forged in seekers' groups, but they emerge out of the common pool of meaning rather than from an argument that has a winner and a loser.

For seekers' groups to thrive, members must maintain pliability in the dialogue, that is, the ability to bend with ideas and people long enough for the life that is hidden in the conversation to emerge. Instead of reacting immediately to something we disagree with, being pliable allows us to go along with ideas and people. Pliability is the precursor to and result of suspension. The more pliable I am, the more I can suspend judgments. The more I suspend judgment, the more pliable I become in future conversations. This is critical to the seekers' group and the seeker's way. Without pliability, my life and my group are destined for rigidity, or worse.

As I learn to bend with ideas and people, and they with me, a wonderful dynamic surfaces: we discover the vein of life hidden in our words. Like excavators, we dig our way to a lode of rich and sacred meaning that can change us all and energize the group. This is one of the most powerful dynamics I've ever been a part of. When my seekers' group finds, through the dialogue, a vein of meaning that prior to our meeting was hidden from us all, the moment is electric. We have found the seeker's path together, and it strengthens us for our individual journeys as well.

∿ Share Your Story ∿

The most important advice I can give you is to let your group take on its own quality as you meet. Your group will probably look different from anything I can even imagine. Wonderful. I hope to hear stories of seekers' groups that are changing each other and the world because of their own creative and unique nature. I have created a Web site for this very purpose. If you're interested in more information on how to start a group, or you would like to share the story of your group with me and others, go to www.theseekersway.com. I look forward to hearing from you.

Live the Mystery.

NOTES

1. Albom, M. *The Five People You Meet in Heaven.* New York: Hyperion, 2003.
2. Isaac, B. *Dialogue and the Art of Thinking.* New York: Doubleday, 1999.

The Author

D ave Fleming is a spiritual mentor and leadership coach, with a Doctor of Management in Organizational Leadership from the University of Phoenix. After twenty years in pastoral ministry, Dave now helps organizations and individuals maximize their potential to better serve the world around them. A contributor to and columnist for Leonard Sweet's Web site, preachingplus.com, Dave is author of *Leadership Wisdom from Unlikely Voices: People of Yesterday Speak to Leaders of Today* (Zondervan, 2004), and has written for a number of leading magazines and journals, including *REV* and *Strategy and Leadership*. Visit Dave's Web sites, www.davefleming.org and www.theseeker'sway.org.

This page constitutes a continuation of the copyright page.

"The Art of Disappearing" from *Words Under the Words: Selected Poems* by Naomi Shihab Nye, copyright © 1995. Reprinted with the permission of Far Corner Books, Portland, Oregon.

Excerpt from "Now I Become Myself," from COLLECTED POEMS 1930–1993 by May Sarton. Copyright © 1993, 1988, 1984, 1980, 1974 by May Sarton. Used by permission of W. W. Norton & Company, Inc.

Other Books of Interest

If you enjoyed this book,
you may be interested in these other
recent titles from Jossey-Bass and Wiley.

**Reimagining Christianity:
Reconnect Your Spirit Without
Disconnecting Your Mind**
Alan Jones
Cloth
ISBN: 0–471–45707–8

"From his pulpit at Grace Cathedral in San Francisco, Alan Jones has influenced for good an entire continent of struggling Christians. In this provoking and helpful new book, he extends his voice to those both within and beyond the Church. A thinking Christian in a thoughtless world is what he is and what he aims to make us. This is a very good start."
— The Reverend Professor Peter J. Gomes, The Memorial Church, Harvard University, and author of *The Good Book*

"Here is a book for all who suspect that God is greater than religion, who regard imagination as a spiritual path, and who could use a wise companion on the way."
— The Rev. Dr. Barbara Brown Taylor, Episcopal priest, author, teacher, and lecturer

In this provocative new book, the internationally renowned Dean of the Episcopal Grace Cathedral in San Francisco delivers a resonant and comforting message to anyone looking for spiritual solace in today's troubled world. Dr. Jones inspires you to think, to question, to dig deeper into the truths of existence as a way of deepening your spirituality rather than accepting rigid dogma. Drawing on his vast knowledge of history, religion, and the heart, Jones encourages you to open doors to those of all faiths and even to those who profess no faith at all. As you do so, you can better understand the powerful promise of Christianity.

Alan Jones, Ph.D., is an Episcopal priest and the dean of Grace Cathedral in San Francisco, California. He lectures all over the world as well as on the Webby Award—nominated gracecathedral.org. Dr. Jones's books include *Seasons of Grace: The Life-Giving Practice of Gratitude,* winner of the prestigious 2004 Nautilus Award in the spirituality category.

A Hidden Wholeness:
The Journey Toward an Undivided Life
Parker J. Palmer
Hardcover
ISBN: 0–7879–7100–6

A BookSense Pick, September 2004

"This book is a treasure—an inspiring, useful blueprint for building safe places where people can commit to "act in every situation in ways that honor the soul."

—*Publishers Weekly*

"The soul is generous: it takes in the needs of the world. The soul is wise: it suffers without shutting down. The soul is hopeful: it engages the world in ways that keep opening our hearts. The soul is creative: it finds its way between realities that might defeat us and fantasies that are mere escapes. All we need to do is to bring down the wall that separates us from our own souls and deprives the world of the soul's regenerative powers."

–From *A Hidden Wholeness*

At a time when many of us seek ways of working and living that are more resonant with our souls, *A Hidden Wholeness* offers insight into our condition and guidance for finding what we seek—within ourselves and with each other.

Parker J. Palmer is a highly respected writer, lecturer, teacher, and activist. His work speaks deeply to people from many walks of life, including public schools, colleges and universities, religious institutions, corporations, foundations, and grass-roots organizations. The Leadership Project, a 1998 survey of 10,000 American educators, named him one of the thirty most influential senior leaders in higher education and one of ten key "agenda-setters" of the past decade. Author of six previous books–including the best-sellers *Let Your Life Speak* and *The Courage to Teach*–his writing has been recognized with eight honorary doctorates and several national awards. He holds a Ph.D. from the University of California at Berkeley and lives in Madison, Wisconsin.

So Much More:
An Invitation to Christian Spirituality
Debra Rienstra
Cloth
ISBN: 0–7879–6887–0

"*So Much More* is a radiant manifesto for the fully realized Christian life. Rienstra speaks to the heart without mawkishness, speaks to the mind without logic-chopping, and speaks to the doubtful without patronizing. With good humor, and with erudition worn lightly, Rienstra provides a compelling Christian account of sin and grace, reason and revelation, the longing for God, the mystery of suffering, and the pathways of love and service."

–Carol Zaleski, professor of religion, Smith College

What does it truly mean to live as a Christian? This intimate, engaging, and beautifully written book speaks to the heart of Christian faith and experience rather than to any one branch or theological position. Debra Rienstra weaves her own experiences as a Christian into chapters on central topics such as transcendence, prayer, churchgoing, the Bible, sin and salvation, and suffering. This is a book for people who don't have all the answers, those who are still thoughtfully considering the depth and breadth of their faith and would like an evocative and sympathetic companion to accompany them on their journey.

Debra Rienstra is a professor of English at Calvin College and the author of *Great with Child: Reflections on Faith, Fullness, and Becoming a Mother.* She lives in Grand Rapids, Michigan.

**If Grace is so Amazing,
Why Don't We Like It?**
Donald McCullough
Cloth
ISBN: 0–7879–7437–4

"Don McCullough is a person with a deep spiritual hunger, and a depth of understanding and challenge that I always find tough, and touching, and illuminating."
–Anne Lamott, author of *Traveling Mercies*

". . . The author looks the issue in the eye with clarity and humor, showing us that our freedom and joy depend on a truth-telling that exposes not only our weakness and fragility but also the breathtaking grace of God that rescues us from despair and makes us radiant with God's delight."
–Alan Jones is the dean of Grace Cathedral, San Francisco,
He is the author of several books. The most recent is
*Reimagining Christianity: Reconnect Your Spirit
Without Disconnecting Your Mind.*

Our instinctive reaction is to pull back from grace. But what does it mean to accept grace for ourselves, to relinquish patterns of wallowing in guilt and instead revel in freedom? With his characteristic humor and warmth, along with a wealth of Biblical and real-life stories, Donald McCullough challenges Christians to understand God's radical grace and what it means to embrace it. He shows how to recognize and extend grace to our relationships–to forgive, to include, and to break down barriers–and thus do the work of Christ on Earth.

Don McCullough (Escondido, CA) is a former president and professor of theology and preaching at San Francisco Theological Seminary. The author of seven books, his writing has appeared in *Christianity Today, Christian Century,* and many other magazines and journals.

White China:
Finding the Divine in the Everyday
Molly Wolf
Foreword by Phyllis Tickle
Cloth
ISBN: 0–7879–6580–4

"White china" is Molly Wolf's personal short-hand for the kind of religious language and ideas that often seem abstract and daunting. Those of us who don't already know them are left to struggle in a landscape of abstraction and purity, intimidated and uncomfortable with our ability to handle them. We might mispronounce the words or use them wrongly, and then what would people think of us? They're pure white china—we might get them dirty. We might drop and break them. And they certainly aren't something we can consume—who can eat china?

In this beautifully written collection of essays, Wolf takes the language of Christian faith and religion, sets it in the context of her keen observations of everyday experience, and unpacks it, opening it up to make it real and close up and important. This charming, quirky, and highly personal book is for those who yearn to be touched, to find meaning, and to deepen their faith through fresh literary explorations of the places where faith meets life.

Molly Wolf (Kingston, Ontario) is the founder of the Web site SabbathBlessings.com and author of *Hiding in Plain Sight; A Place Like any Other; Angels and Dragons: On Sorrow, God, and Healing*; and *Knitlit* and *Knitlit (Too)*, both with Linda Roghaar.

Finding Our Way Home:
Turning Back to What Matters Most
Mark R. McMinn
Cloth
ISBN: 0–7879–7531–1

"In some quarters, Christians have a reputation for being deathly afraid of diversity, conflict, humor, sexuality, and most of the other things that help make life worth living. Here is a book to prove it need not be so. Mark McMinn writes honestly, movingly, and well from his rich immersion in life, exploring experiences we can all identify with and finding the dimension of depth hidden in them. He helps us to understand the enlivening and liberating meaning of 'the Word became flesh and dwelt among us, full of grace and truth.'"

—Parker J. Palmer, author of *A Hidden Wholeness,*
Let Your Life Speak, and *The Courage to Teach.*

"We are all caught within the confusing and contradictory swirl of emotions like love and hate, hope and despair, remembering and forgetfulness, loathing and longing. Mark McMinn pointedly reveals that what so ruthlessly and lovingly draws them all together is the deep gravitational pull of home."

—Michael Card, musician and author of
A Fragile Stone and *Scribbling in the Sand*

Written in an intimate, personal style, *Finding Our Way Home* draws on the powerful insights of psychology, Christian spirituality, and theology to explore the human longing for a home, a spiritual as much as a physical place where we are at peace with ourselves and with God. McMinn asks readers to consider the different aspects of home as a spiritual metaphor–what we grew up in as well as the challenges of living well within our present realities–and in the process he addresses the yearning for a spiritual center, a deeper relationship with God, and peace in our lives.

Mark McMinn (Winfield, IL) is Rech Professor of Psychology at Wheaton College where he also initiated and directs the Center for Church-Psychology Collaboration. He has authored over 100 journal articles and chapters and seven books, including *Why Sin Matters* (Tyndale, 2004).

Seasons of a Restless Heart: A Spiritual Companion for Living in Transition
Debra Farrington
Cloth
ISBN: 0–7879–7392–0

"In this work, Debra Farrington has done a beautiful job of Christian interpretation by building a bridge between the ancient stories of the Exodus and our contemporary experiences of transition. She shares most eloquently what she has learned from others, and more importantly, what she has experienced personally. Her words will both enlighten and inspire."

—John R. Claypool, Episcopal priest and author of *The Hopeful Heart*

"Debra Farrington has always been a deeply practical, realistic, and honest writer whose work is companionable and full of stories. In *The Seasons of a Restless Heart* she is all these things and much, much more. In 'the times between ending and beginning,' Farrington finds the poetry as well as the agony of change; and in the act of reporting on them, she allays our fears and charms our spirits back to faith, hope, and—yes—to charity. This is the handbook of choice for every life in transit."

—Phyllis Tickle, author of *The Divine Hours*

Popular retreat leader and author Debra Farrington uses the story of the Israelites and their time spent in the desert, before they reached the Promised Land, to illuminate the challenges of letting go of the past in order to move on to the future. Focusing not on grieving the past or creating the future, but rather on the time in between as a period of rest, play, creativity, and discernment, she details a spiritual approach to times of transition, encouraging readers to ask what God desires for them and how they can use this in-between time to move closer to God.

Debra K. Farrington (Hershey, PA) is a wise writer, popular retreat leader, and publishing insider with a growing following. She is currently vice president of Morehouse Publishing, was manager of the Graduate Theological Union Bookstore in Berkeley, California, and has published in a wide variety of publications including *Spirituality and Health, Catholic Digest, Alive Now, U.S. Catholic Magazine, The Lutheran, Publishers Weekly,* and many others. This is her sixth book.